The Physics of Miraculous Healing is a revolutionary, life-changing read. It offers a powerful bridge for the soul's healing wisdom to transform us physically, emotionally, and spiritually. A new life can await anyone who sincerely studies its beautifully crafted message integrating quantum physics, healing, and spirituality. I loved this book!—**Joseph Bharat Cornell**, author of *AUM: The Melody of Love* and *Sharing Nature*

This is an interesting addition to the growing literature on mind-body healing. The book is very readable and recommended.—**Amit Goswami**, PhD, Author of the *Quantum Doctor*, and, with **Dr. Onisor**, of *Quantum Integrative Medicine*.

The Physics of Miraculous Healing is a significant theoretical and practical contribution to extending our understanding of this well-attested and largely neglected phenomenon. Given that such phenomena do occur, we must advance plausible explanatory hypotheses to account for them, which molecular medicine - based on classical physics - is manifestly unable to do. Selbie's innovative approach draws on M-theory, non-locality, the holographic paradigm, subtle energy bodies and the operation of a higher spiritual intelligence in coherently repatterning the body template. The author also includes key practices that we can all implement to align ourselves and optimise our health on every level. Highly recommended reading.—**David Lorimer**, *Founder of The Science and Medical Network and Chair of the Galileo Commission*

Miraculous events are not really outside the realm of human experience, as the stories in this book clearly demonstrate. Nor are they inexplicable, or random, when you delve deeply enough into the subtle laws of the universe. Brilliant. Profound. These superlatives accurately define the first half of the book. What comes next is a remarkable handbook of how to put yourself in tune with these subtle laws so as to manifest in your own life the same remarkable possibilities. First half incentivises the reader to begin to practice what the second half of the book explains in simple, practical, I-can-do-this terms. A life-changing read.—**Asha Nayaswami**, author of *Lightbearer*, speaker, meditator

The Physics of Miraculous Healing is foundational in joining the fields of medicine, physics, and metaphysics to create a new paradigm for optimal health and well-being. Selbie is a gifted writer who is able to explain subtle, esoteric principles of both science and metaphysics in clear, cogent ways that everyone can easily understand. We can't speak highly enough of this groundbreaking work that shows a new approach to healing for the future.—**Nayaswami Jyotish & Nayaswami Devi**, *Spiritual Directors of Ananda Worldwide*

Selbie masterfully elucidates the frontier revelations of vanguard sciences…with the universal features of mystical experience. Physical, emotional, mental and spiritual well-being are our birthright; miraculous healings and superconscious attainments are our destiny!—**Dana Lynne Andersen**, author of *Art and Spirit* and founder of *The Academy of Art, Creativity & Consciousness*

We've all heard stories of spontaneous healings, radical remissions, and miracle recoveries from incurable cancers. But let's be honest, how many of us understand enough about the actual mechanics of miracles to really believe one could happen for us? Now along comes Joseph Selbie with his trademark gift for explaining complex quantum physics topics in a simple, engaging, easy to grasp manner, and suddenly, the light goes on. Louise Hay told us we can heal ourselves. Joseph Selbie made me a believer when he showed me how.—**Sandie Sedgbeer**, Talk TV/Radio host and Founder of the No BS Spiritual Book Club.

The Physics of Miraculous Healing

How Emotion, Mind, and Spirit
Enable Unlimited Self-Healing

JOSEPH SELBIE

Published by
Protectors Press,
Nevada City, CA 95959

Copyright © 2024 by Joseph Selbie

All rights reserved. No part of this publication may be reproduced or transmitted in any form by any means, electronic or mechanical, including photocopying, recording, or by any information storage and retrieval system, without permission in writing from Joseph Selbie. Reviewers may quote brief passages.

ISBN: 978-0-9898052-3-0

Cover design by Phil Dyer

When we begin to understand the total being that is man, we realize that he is no simple physical organism. Within him are many powers whose potential he employs in greater or lesser degree in accommodating himself to the conditions of this world. Their potential is vastly greater than the average person thinks.

—Paramhansa Yogananda

Contents

Introduction...1

Part 1—What is the Body?

Chapter 1—The Body is a Molecular Machine..................10

Chapter 2—The Body is Made of Energy..........................23

Chapter 3—The Body Extends into Another Realm............34

Chapter 4—The Body is Holographic................................44

Chapter 5—The Body is Intelligently Guided....................52

Chapter 6—The Body is a Continuous Miracle..................57

Part 2—Understanding Your Soul Powers

Chapter 7—Emotion...62

Chapter 8—Belief..70

Chapter 9—Connection to Spirit......................................80

Part 3—Practices and Techniques to Access and Use Your Soul Powers for Resilient Health and Self-Healing

Chapter 10—Setting Expectations...................................90

Chapter 11—A Note on Other Healing Modalities.............96

Chapter 12—Awaken and Strengthen Positive Emotions......97

Chapter 13—Increase Your Life Force............................107

Chapter 14—Develop Belief in Unlimited Health............115

Chapter 15—Connect with Spirit................................120

Part 4—How to Meditate and Establish Strong Habits

Chapter 16—How to Meditate...................................127

Chapter 17—How to Establish Strong Habits..................138

Notes...145

Bibliography..152

Acknowledgments...161

About the Author..162

INTRODUCTION

In February 2002 Anita Moorjani was diagnosed with lymphoma, a form of cancer that creates tumors in the lymph glands. She began using alternative methods of healing but, having no success, eventually underwent several conventional cancer treatments. Despite these treatments she became emaciated and weak; she had large visible tumors and open lesions. Her doctors informed her and her family that there was nothing more they could do and sent her to the hospital for her final days or hours.

In the ambulance on her way to the hospital she entered a deep coma that lasted thirty hours. In those thirty hours she had a life-transforming near-death experience during which she realized that a lifetime of deeply felt fear was the root cause of her cancer. She also experienced herself wonderfully free, filled by and immersed in an infinite ocean of unconditional love. She understood that she, herself, was that love—and that love was her cure.

> We are pure love—every single one of us. I knew that realizing this meant never being afraid of who we are. As I experienced my biggest revelation, it felt like a bolt of lightning. I understood that merely by being the love I truly am, I would heal both myself and others. [During the experience she was told] now that you know the

The Physics of Miraculous Healing

truth of who you really are, go back and live your life fearlessly!—Anita Moorjani, author of *Dying to Be Me*[1]

Anita's near-death experience ended and she came out of her coma. Alert and vibrant, she rallied rapidly. Within four days her tumors shrank by 70%; at five weeks, she was free of any signs of cancer and on her way home from the hospital.

In 1957, Mr. Wright was a hospital cancer patient of Dr. Phillip West in Long Beach, California. He had lympho-sarcoma. His lungs were filled with fluid, and malignant tumors "the size of oranges" were visible on his neck, chest, and abdomen. His condition was considered inoperable, untreatable, and terminal. He was told he had just two weeks to live.

At about this time, Mr. Wright read that a new wonder drug to treat cancer such as his—Krebiozen—was being tested in the hospital where he was a patient. Feeling highly optimistic about the drug, he was determined to have it given to him. Though he was told that he didn't qualify to be in the test because his cancer was too advanced, he continued to demand treatment until Dr. West finally agreed to include him in the test group.

Dr. West injected Mr. Wright with a dose of Krebiozen on a Friday afternoon. "I had left him febrile, gasping for air, completely bedridden," Dr. West wrote. To his amazement, by Monday Mr. Wright's tumors "had melted like snowballs on a hot stove." *Yet no other patients who had received Krebiozen had shown any improvement.* A baffled Dr. West continued to administer the injections. Ten days after the first injection, his health fully restored, Mr. Wright left the hospital and flew himself home in his own plane.

Two months later Mr. Wright read multiple medical reports stating that Krebiozen was proving to be ineffective. His health deteriorated rapidly and he had to return to the hospital. Dr. West took a bold risk, which today would be considered unethical, and told him there was a "new super-refined double strength" version of Krebiozen coming to the hospital in the next few days.

Ill as he was, Mr. Wright became his optimistic self again, eager to start over. Dr. West delayed two days before telling Mr. Wright that the nonexistent "shipment" had arrived, intentionally increasing his anticipation. By then, Mr. Wright was almost ecstatic; his belief very strong. With much fanfare, Dr. West administered the first injection of what was simply a saline solution. Recovery from Mr. Wright's second near-terminal state was even more dramatic than the first. In only days, tumor masses melted, chest fluid vanished, Mr. Wright became ambulatory, and even went back to flying again.

Some months later, alas, Mr. Wright read yet another report declaring that Krebiozen was not at all effective as a cancer treatment. He once again succumbed to cancer. Within two days he died.[2]

In 1965 Barbara Cummiskey, then fifteen years old, began showing symptoms of multiple sclerosis. Multiple sclerosis is a central nervous system disorder that causes a wide variety of debilitating conditions and is believed to be incurable. Though lovingly cared for by her parents, by the time she was thirty-one, she had twice come close to death when her heart and lungs failed; her hands and feet were so unnaturally and tightly curled that she could not walk or perform most tasks with her hands; she was functionally blind; she no longer had urinary or bowel control; one lung had collapsed and her diaphragm was partially paralyzed; she needed extra oxygen at all times; and she needed to be helped into a wheelchair in order to go outside her room.

Despite this litany of disabilities, Barbara remained clear in her mind and determined in her heart. She realized that though she had lost many physical abilities, she still had the ability to pray for others. Every day she spent hours praying for people. As she prayed, she felt closer to God; often she talked to God as if He were standing near.

The Physics of Miraculous Healing

By 1981, as her condition steadily worsened, her family accepted that she had only a short time left and prepared her for hospice care. On June 7, the day of her sister's birthday party, Barbara wanted to do something special for her. Her mother helped her out of bed and into her wheelchair, hooked up her oxygen and wheeled her to the kitchen. There with great effort Barbara barely managed to give a few stirs to the cake batter for her sister's cake.

That evening, talking with friends in her room, she heard a voice inaudible to anyone else: "My child, get up and walk!" To her astonishment—and everyone else's—she unhooked herself from all the devices that had been keeping her body alive. Then she stood up. She felt tingling all over. She could breathe fully; her hands and feet had returned to normal; her arms and legs were filled out and whole. Walking into the living room she performed a few ballet steps she hadn't been able to do for sixteen years. A visit to her doctor the next day confirmed that her multiple sclerosis was completely gone.

> I don't know why God healed me. I don't believe I 'earned' or 'deserved' a healing any more than I 'deserved' MS. I only know that on the morning of June 7, 1981, I felt good about myself—mentally, emotionally, and spiritually well. Through my prayer life, I was a busy, active member of the human family—not running or jumping or even walking like most people, but not separated from them by bitterness, self-pity, or despair. My mind and spirit were healthy and whole. And then God made my body whole, too.—Barbara Cummiskey[3]

These dramatic cases show clearly that people *can* recover from any condition or disease, even those considered incurable and terminal, and that extraordinarily rapid, even instantaneous, physical change is possible. Cases such as these are often termed "miraculous" simply because they have no scientific explanation.

The Physics of Miraculous Healing

Other cases are termed miraculous because the person healed personally experienced divine intervention. However we view these cases, they clearly suggest that there is much more to healing than is presently understood by modern medicine.

Not only do such extraordinarily rapid, even instantaneous, miraculous healings take place, they do so far more often than most people realize. The Institute of Noetic Sciences' Caryle Hirshberg, Ph.D., a former Stanford biochemist, combed through Western medical records and found *over fifteen hundred verified cases* of people unexplainably healed from terminal cancer and other diseases considered incurably fatal. Dr. Hirshberg compiled her findings in the book, *Spontaneous Remissions: An Annotated Bibliography*.

Spontaneous remissions from cancer, and other extraordinary healings of incurable diseases with no scientific explanation, are only the first type of "miracle." There are equally well-documented examples of extraordinary healing in which the person healed was actively praying for divine aid.

The Medical Bureau for the Sanctuary of Lourdes is made up of a team of highly reputable doctors—including, at one time, a Nobel Prize-winner—who minutely review instances of miraculous healing among visitors to Lourdes. In the decades since the Medical Bureau began its work, the team of doctors has verified seventy cases of miraculous healing. Seventy cases may not seem an impressive number until we consider the stringent criteria used: there must first be a verified and unfavorable prognosis of a serious disease; there must be objective, biological, radiological evidence of the disease; there cannot have been any other treatment undertaken by the sufferer that could account for a cure; *recovery must be sudden, instantaneous, immediate and without convalescence;* and finally, the cure must be complete, lasting, and definitive.[4]

Despite the impressive quality of data, modern medicine generally ignores verified cases of extraordinarily rapid, miraculous healing because they fall outside of what can be explained by modern medicine. Turning a blind eye to such remarkable results, alas, leaves a vast potential untapped.

> Even if they hardly ever happen, these 'miracles' are the kinds of exceptions to the ruling paradigm that inevitably create new areas of study.—James Gordon, M.D., Georgetown Medical School professor and director of the Center for Mind-Body Studies[5]
>
> If several hundred patients have succeeded in doing this sort of thing, eliminating vast numbers of malignant cells on their own, the possibility that medicine can learn to accomplish the same thing at will is surely within the reach of imagining.—Lewis Thomas, The Youngest Science: Notes of a Medicine Watcher[6]

Such "imagining," however, is difficult to achieve within the confining boundaries of current medical theory. Biological laws, which are the foundation of modern medicine, *fundamentally rule out the possibility* that miraculous healing can occur. There simply are no biological laws that can explain how extraordinarily rapid physical change is possible. Lacking scientific validation, doctors lean toward assuming that reported cases have either been poorly diagnosed or put forward with fraudulent intent.

Such "imagining" is made doubly difficult to accept within current medical theory because those healed attribute their healing to many practices that aren't *material*, the chosen domain of medical research. Among those non-material practices are releasing negative emotions and increasing positive emotions; examining and changing core beliefs; and making an inner connection to Spirit.

Which brings us to the three purposes of this book:

- One, to show that science *does* support miraculous healing, that while the laws of modern medicine and biology are at a loss to explain extraordinarily rapid physiological change there are other branches of science, notably within physics, that do support such change.

- Two, to show how and why non-material practices, such as developing positive emotions, changing what one believes, or making a connection to Spirit, can affect the physical body.
- Three, to show that the keys to miraculous healing are also the keys to everyday health and that these keys are within everyone's reach.

Current biological laws are based on what is known as *classical physics,* a discipline that was firmly established by the late 1800s. The laws of classical physics are matter-centered; atoms and molecules are viewed as *unchangeable bits of matter.* Modern medicine uses these same laws of classical physics that can explain how a car engine works to explain how a human body works.

By the early 1900s, however, newer disciplines within physics began to emerge. *Modern physics,* as these newer disciplines are now generally known, has a fundamentally different view of reality from classical physics. The laws of modern physics are energy-centered; atoms and molecules are viewed not as unchangeable bits of matter but as *changeable organized patterns of energy* and there are now disciplines on the frontiers of modern physics that provide support for how *nonphysical* influences such as emotions, beliefs, or prayer can have a direct transformative effect on the *physical* body.

Some disciplines on the frontiers of physics are also highly congruent with millennia-old spiritual traditions, such as Vedic spirituality, mystical Christianity, Buddhism, Sufism, Kabbalah, and Daoism. When these two views of reality—energy physics and metaphysics—are considered together, they provide a bridge between science and spirituality without any loss of scientific rigor; they provide a mechanism through which Spirit can operate without breaking the laws of science. Far from ruling *out* the possibility of Spirit, theories on the frontiers of physics rule *in* the possibility, even making a case for the necessity of Spirit.

The Physics of Miraculous Healing

> The first gulp from the glass of natural sciences will turn you into an atheist, but at the bottom of the glass God is waiting for you.—Werner Heisenberg, Nobel Prize-winner in physics[7]
>
> There probably is a God. Many things are easier to explain if there is than if there isn't.—John Von Neumann, physicist and mathematician[8]

Cases of extraordinarily rapid, miraculous healing indicate that we have access to a vast potential for self-healing. Tapping into this vast healing potential is achieved by discovering and learning to use our innate self-healing powers. Our innate self-healing powers are the key to both extraordinarily rapid, miraculous healing and every day health because, in a very real way, our bodies are continuous miracles.

Part 1

What is the Body?

CHAPTER 1—The Body is a Molecular Machine

In the introduction I stated that there simply are no laws in matter-centered, classical physics-based biology that can explain extraordinarily rapid physical change but that the laws of energy-centered, modern physics can. Let's first look at why biology's laws *can't* explain extraordinarily rapid physical change in order to understand how the laws of modern physics *can*.

Most people believe that the body is made of atoms and molecules and that interactions between those atoms and molecules enable the body to function as an extremely complex *molecular machine*.

This widely embraced view of the body comes directly from modern medicine. Medicine's view is based on the twin foundations of biochemistry and molecular biology, both of which are based on classical physics. From a young age most of us have been exposed to the basic principles of these disciplines and their principles are continuously reinforced by doctors, biochemists, drug companies, books, magazines, advertising, the internet, and even the news.

There is no denying the success of modern medicine's molecular-machine approach to treating the body. Modern drugs, surgery, and trauma care—the primary practices of modern medicine—have saved millions of lives and greatly extended life expectancy. The success of the molecular-machine model of the body has made most doctors and, indeed, most people, highly confident that all functions of the body and all healing are solely the result of molecular interactions. To appreciate why, let's look at how modern medicine describes the key parts of its molecular machine and how those parts work together.

Biomolecules

Biomolecules are the essential building blocks of the molecular machine. A molecule is nothing more than two or more atoms bonded together and biomolecules are simply molecules created in living organisms.

Among the many types of biomolecules identified by biochemistry, proteins are the workhorses. Proteins bond together to provide the structure of the body. They are also essential to nearly every complex molecular interaction enabling the numerous life-processes that maintain the body, from digestion to immune response.

It is estimated that the human body produces as many as two million different types of proteins. Amino acids, small molecules themselves, are the Lego brick-like building blocks of all proteins because amino acids will readily connect to each other to form long chains. As amino acids are connected to build a protein, the lengthening chain folds back on itself in ways unique to each protein. The unique folding of each protein's amino acid chain results in a unique final shape. The unique final shape of the protein determines its function.

DNA

DNA is the most complex molecule in the human body. DNA contains unique sequences of four nucleotides—adenine (A), thymine (T), guanine (G), and cytosine (C). These unique sequences of A, T, G, and C are the templates which guide the creation of the two million different proteins put to work in the human body.

The Physics of Miraculous Healing

Often said to be the brain of the cell, DNA has long been believed to be encoded with instructions that direct and regulate all of a cell's internal functions, as well as enabling the cell to play its cooperative part in essential life-processes that determine the body's health from birth to death.

The Cell

The adult human body is composed of forty to sixty trillion cells. Common to all cells in the human body are three essential functions: they allow atoms or molecules in or out through their membranes; they make proteins; and they transform glucose and oxygen into useable energy. Cells are not all the same. Cells have specialized functions to make up particular tissues such as lung, muscle, or connective tissue. The body grows and is maintained by cells dividing in two. The two resulting cells are exact copies of each other.

Protein Production

Cells are sometimes referred to as protein factories. Every cell in the body produces an enormous number of proteins. The process begins with DNA in the cell's nucleus unwinding its double-helix to expose a specific protein-template sequence which enables the DNA's protein-template sequence to be copied in a new strand of messenger RNA. Once formed, the messenger RNA strand makes its way out of the nucleus to bind with one of the cell's approximately ten million ribosomes. Ribosomes can be thought of as amino acid-connecting micro-machines. Once bound to a ribosome, messenger RNA provides the physical template that enables the ribosome to connect amino acids in the precise sequence needed to form a specific usable protein.

ATP Production

ATP is a molecule that functions as a tiny battery; it releases its single positive electrochemical charge to enable myriad

The Physics of Miraculous Healing

cellular processes including protein production. Protein production requires one or two electrochemical charges to connect each amino acid to the next. ATP molecules are produced by the trillions in the thousands of mitochondria within each cell. Mitochondria transform glucose—an end product of the digestive process—and oxygen—which is brought into the body as we breathe—into the battery-like ATP molecules.

Protein Messengers

Cells frequently interact with other cells in the multicellular human body. Protein messengers, such as hormones and neurotransmitters, introduced into the bloodstream by cells, can influence the behavior of other cells by *binding* with a specialized receptor-protein situated on the outer membrane of another cell. The mechanics of the binding process is often explained by analogy with a lock and key: a uniquely shaped protein, such as a neurotransmitter, is the protein-key; and the uniquely shaped protein-key can fit only a uniquely shaped receptor protein-lock.

When a messenger protein-key inserts itself into a receptor protein-lock one of two things can happen: 1. specific life-processes can be *stimulated* by a messenger protein-key that initiates a cascade of chemical interactions within the cell or 2. specific cellular functions can be *inhibited* by the messenger protein-key by it simply occupying the protein-lock but not initiating any chemical interactions.

Drugs

Protein-keys and receptor protein-locks, and the dynamics of chemical messenger functioning, are a foundation of pharmacology. Most pharmaceutical drugs are *artificially* produced protein-keys that fit into *naturally* occurring protein-receptor locks. Drugs stimulate or inhibit life-processes that are not already being stimulated or inhibited by the natural production of the body's own protein-keys.

The Physics of Miraculous Healing

The Brain and Nervous System

Nervous system cells, known as neurons, act as tiny wires through which a micro-voltage can electrochemically pass in order to stimulate other neurons. Neurons also produce protein messengers such as neurotransmitters that stimulate activity in many kinds of cells by binding with receptor-proteins on their surfaces. These two functions, chemical signaling accomplished through protein messengers binding with receptor sites, or electrochemical signaling accomplished through micro-voltage passing from one neuron to the next, are the communication methods used by the brain and nervous system to initiate or stimulate life-processes, receive sensory input, and coordinate physical movement.

Putting It All Together

It's easy to see why many scientists believe that the body is a molecular machine: Precisely shaped proteins give structure to the body. DNA, containing a master set of protein templates, opens its coils to allow one specific protein template to be copied in RNA form. Ribosomes, molecular assembly micro-machines, connect amino acids in precise sequence to produce proteins according to an RNA template. Mitochondria produce tiny molecular batteries that enable the bonding of two amino acids like a weld that bonds two pieces of metal. Precisely shaped protein-keys find and fit into precisely shaped protein-locks to block or pass on molecular messages. Neurons, like electric wires, send signals throughout the body.

It is also no secret that most doctors, biochemists, and molecular biologists are confident that not only is the body a molecular machine but that the molecular machine model has, or soon will have, all the answers to every function of the body.

The Physics of Miraculous Healing

Major Flaws in the Molecular-Machine Model

Ironically, given such widespread confidence, the molecular machine model has no answers to how two of the most basic and vital functions of the body—ultra-fast intra-cellular activity and body-wide coordination of all life-processes—can occur. In fact:

1. A molecular machine has *inherent speed limits* that prevent it from achieving the speeds of intra-cellular activity, such as protein production, that it must achieve to in order to be a viable organism.
2. The molecular machine has *no molecular mechanisms* to coordinate the astonishingly complex and rapid cellular-level life-processes that happen within each cell and in concert with every other cell.

These are major flaws because, not only can they not currently be explained by the molecular-machine model, they are beyond what a molecular machine can do.

The Molecular Machine's Speed Limits

There is a significant disconnect between the estimates of how many proteins need to be produced each day to support a healthy adult body and the estimates of how fast purely machine-like processes in the cells can produce those proteins. In order to create new cells to replace damaged ones, to maintain the structure of healthy cells, and to produce all the proteins needed to enable essential life-processes such as digestion, metabolism, and immune response, every one of the forty to sixty trillion cells in the adult body needs to produce approximately 11,000 proteins—every second—continuously, night and day, from birth to death. In a typical twenty-four-hour day, all the cells in the body must combine to produce *sextillions* of proteins—a number that rivals the number of stars in the universe.

If the body was indeed solely a molecular machine, it would not be possible for it to create that many proteins in a single day. All machines have speed limits. A car with an internal combustion, piston engine can go only so fast, and no faster. The

The Physics of Miraculous Healing

speed at which fuel can enter the cylinder and the speed a piston can physically move up and down, place an upper limit on engine speed, and thus an upper limit on the speed the car can go.

A discipline within biology known as *biophysics* applies to the body the basic laws of classical physics. When those laws are applied to the molecular-machine functions of the body, serious doubts arise whether molecular-machine functions can perform rapidly enough to produce the number of proteins the body does, in fact, produce.

The average cell has ten million protein-producing ribosomes. Once the beginning of an RNA protein-template strand enters a ribosome, the ribosome begins to connect specific amino acids in sequence that exactly match the sequence of the RNA protein-template strand. When the process is complete, the ribosome releases both the RNA protein-template strand and the finished protein into the cell's cytoplasm and begins the process anew to create another protein with a new strand of RNA.

Amino acid chains that form proteins can be as long as thirty thousand amino acids, such as *titin*, a key protein in muscle fiber, although most proteins are in the range of hundreds of amino acids in length. Taking a low average of two hundred amino acids per protein, it would require every one of the ten million ribosomes in a cell to continuously connect amino acids at an average of *five amino acids per second* for that cell to produce a total of eleven-thousand proteins per second. The current estimate in biophysics, however, which looks at the process simply from the point of view of the mechanical laws of classical physics, is that a ribosome, at best, can connect an average of little *over three amino acids per second*.[1]

This might not seem to be a very big disconnect. One might think that the discrepancy may simply be caused by various under- or over-estimations regarding the required number of proteins and the number of available ribosomes. However, there is a significant caveat to the three-amino-acid pace projected by biophysicists: maintaining that pace is only possible *if* both the

RNA template strand and exactly the right numbers of each of twenty different kinds of amino acid needed to make a protein are *immediately adjacent* to the ribosome. To maintain that pace, even for one ribosome, let alone all ten million in a single cell, or the quadrillions in all cells combined, there can be absolutely no time delays caused by the right amino acid not being near the ribosome at the precise instant it is needed.

There is little likelihood, however, that the right amino acids will, in fact, *always* be available to a ribosome at the precise instant they are needed. No molecular mechanism is known that can ensure that all the raw materials for a given protein will *always* be immediately adjacent to the ribosome. According to known molecular behavior, RNA templates and amino acids can only float around randomly in the semi-liquid cytoplasm of the cell.

Even if each ribosome could in some way attract the right amino acids to it while producing a protein, those amino acids would still require time to make their way to the ribosome. Even if the time required were as little as fractions of a second, the net result would be that the actual pace of protein production would be significantly reduced.

The realistic pace of connecting amino acids for each ribosome, when we factor in the problem of amino acid availability and adjacency, is likely far less than three amino acids per second per ribosome. This makes the disconnect between the number of proteins the body does produce each day and the number of proteins the molecular machine is capable of producing even greater.

Even if there were such mechanisms or molecular behaviors ensuring that every ribosome could draw the right amino acids to it the instant it needs it to make a specific protein, and even if ribosomes could continuously maintain their highest pace of protein production, every second of every day, from birth to death, once we factor in extraordinarily rapid physical change, such as Barbara Cummiskey's substantial and almost instantaneous change, molecular-machine production of

The Physics of Miraculous Healing

proteins could not even remotely keep pace with the numbers of proteins needed.

Physical change at the speed and scale of Barbara Cummiskey's healing—billions of nerve cells repaired, internal organs remade, tens of pounds of new muscle mass added—would require the creation of trillions upon trillions of completely *new cells*, which in turn would require the sextillions of proteins that the body normally creates in a full twenty-four hours, to be created in minutes or moments—a transformation impossible for a body, functioning solely as a molecular machine, to accomplish. It would be as if a car capable of going one hundred miles per hour suddenly began to go ten thousand miles per hour.

There is little doubt that the molecular machine behavior of the body does occur; that behavior simply can't be the *only* behavior of which the body is capable. There must be other laws at work that can explain the astonishing pace of not only routine protein production but also the pace of protein production necessary for extraordinarily rapid physical change.

What Coordinates the Molecular Machine?

It is little known or appreciated—yet extremely significant—that there are no mechanisms within the molecular machine that can explain how the mindboggling number of life-processes that routinely occur across trillions of cells every second of every day are *coordinated*.

It has been estimated that every second within the average cell, fifty-thousand coordinated sequences of molecular interaction simultaneously take place—DNA opens its coils to allow the formation of RNA protein templates, amino acids are stitched together to create one of two million different types of proteins, ATP batteries are both created and used, and channels constantly open in the cell membrane to allow raw materials, such as glucose and amino acids, into the cell and finished proteins, such as hormones and enzymes, out of the cell. Multiplied by trillions of

The Physics of Miraculous Healing

cells, the total number grows to *quadrillions* of coordinated sequences of molecular interaction taking place in the human body *every single second*.

Not only do quadrillions of coordinated sequences of molecular interactions occur every second and sextillions of proteins get produced every day—they are *perfectly coordinated* across forty to sixty trillion cells. For example, the body creates exactly the right proteins—both for every cell and in concert with every cell in the body—at exactly the right moment to allow all the cells in the body to function with exquisite interactive precision. And protein production is but one coordinated sequence of molecular interaction among thousands that must be synchronized with every other sequence of molecular interaction that allows the body to function.

For the last half of the twentieth century, it was believed that the DNA in every cell provides the lion's share of the coordination necessary; that DNA contained not only protein templates but also some kind of programming which could not only minutely coordinate all molecular interactions within a specific cell but do so in synchronous coordination with all the other cells in the body. This programming in our DNA was believed to be so comprehensive that it determined our life span, our general health, the likelihood of our getting terminal illnesses such as cancer, our degree of intelligence, even psychological and emotional traits.

The belief that programming in our DNA provided the lion's share of the coordination of cellular processes, however, came to an abrupt end in 2003 when the Human Genome Project produced the first complete sequencing of the human genetic code. Geneticists had thought that once the entire human genome was sequenced, they would be able to understand all the unexplained mysteries of how the programming in our DNA coordinates the life-processes within every cell and throughout the body as a whole.

The Physics of Miraculous Healing

But it didn't. To their shock, geneticists found *no* programming in the genome for coordinating life-processes.

> When the human genome was sequenced, some scientists were saying, "That's the end. We're going to understand every disease. We're going to understand every behavior." And it turns out, we didn't, because the sequence of the DNA isn't enough to explain behavior. It isn't enough to explain diseases.—Denise Chow, LiveScience: Why Your DNA May Not Be Your Destiny[2]

To appreciate the implications of the absence of any programming in our DNA, imagine being given a randomly ordered list of the two million different parts required to make a skyscraper—every nut, bolt, and fastener to exact size, every measurement of every part from steel to glass—but not being given a blueprint for the entire building nor any instructions for assembly.

Finding no instructions in our DNA forced geneticists to fundamentally reassess how genes function. This reassessment was complicated further by the relatively recent discoveries of the new discipline known as epigenetics. Epigenetics has shown that genes are not fixed—inactive genes can become active and active genes can become inactive.

Over the course of three months, a group of over thirty men with low-risk prostate cancer, following an intensive regimen focused on nutrition and lifestyle, activated 48 genes that help the body fight tumors and deactivated 453 genes that tend to promote tumors.[3] More amazing yet are the number of epigenetic changes made over a six-month period in a Swedish study of twenty-three slightly overweight men attending spinning and aerobics classes twice per week. Researchers at Lund University discovered that the men had epigenetically altered 7,000 genes![4]

From these and other studies, we now know that environmental, behavioral, mental, and emotional influences can

The Physics of Miraculous Healing

activate thousands of genes once considered permanently deactivated, or deactivate thousands of genes once considered to be permanently active. Twins who begin their lives with identical sets of activated genes can end their lives with significantly different sets of activated genes.

Considering that no programming has been found in human DNA to coordinate all life-processes, the routine activation and deactivation of genes very much suggests that it is the genes that are being coordinated rather than that the genes are doing the coordinating.

The only other possible source of coordination to be found in the molecular machine is the brain and nervous system. But our neurons are simply neither fast enough nor numerous enough to coordinate quadrillions of cellular events every second.

A single round trip message from the brain to a cell and back again can take up to two seconds; protein messengers secreted by neurons in the brain can take up to tens of seconds to make their way through the bloodstream to receptor sites on cells. These speeds are not remotely fast enough for the brain to coordinate even one cell's blindingly fast molecular interactions, let alone trillions of cells simultaneously. Coordinating *all* the body's molecular interactions through the brain and nervous system would be like trying to run all the trades of the New York Stock Exchange—which are coordinated by multiple massive supercomputers—through a single personal computer.

Our nervous system's neural capacity is sufficient to provide macro-control but not micro-control over our life-processes. The brain can send signals through the nerves or release protein messengers into the bloodstream that *influence* macro life-processes, such as switching on or off digestive processes and increasing or decreasing heart rate and circulation, but the limited number of nerve signals or protein messengers the nervous system can produce cannot possibly control all the molecular interactions that occur every second inside our trillions of cells.

To say the lack of mechanisms to coordinate life-processes is a major flaw in the notion that the body is a molecular machine is a vast understatement. Without such coordination, the body simply cannot exist.

The Molecular-Machine Model of the Body is Incomplete

Modern medicine's view of the human body as a molecular machine can't explain the astonishing speed at which fundamental life-processes routinely occur—such as producing sextillion proteins per day—let alone explain instances of extraordinarily rapid change in the physical body, such as was experienced by Anita Moorjani, Mr. Wright, and, especially, Barbara Cummiskey, in whose body trillions of new cells were created in moments. Additionally, modern medicine's molecular-machine model lacks any mechanisms to explain how quadrillions of simultaneous molecular events occurring within trillions of different cells are perfectly coordinated to ensure the body's optimal function.

There is no doubt that the body does function as a molecular machine. A century of experiments and discoveries have shown that molecular-machine behavior occurs in every cell in the body. Yet, just as a car with a top speed of one hundred miles per hour can't suddenly go ten thousand miles per hour, the molecular-machine body can't suddenly and dramatically exceed the limits of the laws that govern molecular-machine behavior. There must be *additional and complementary laws* at work to explain the speed and coordination of the body's functions.

The first set of complementary laws we will explore emerged at the turn of the twentieth century with a revolution in physics that fundamentally changed our view of matter.

CHAPTER 2—The Body is Made of Energy

We know the molecular-machine model of the human body is incomplete because the matter-centered laws of classical physics—on which modern medicine's twin foundations of biochemistry and molecular biology rest—are themselves incomplete. The matter-centered laws of classical physics are incomplete because they don't integrate the more fundamental and more complete energy-centered laws of *relativity and quantum physics*.

Einstein's 1905 special theory of relativity, encapsulated in his famous equation, $E=MC^2$, and the discipline of quantum physics that developed in the decades after, revealed that matter is made of energy. All atoms and molecules, and all the subatomic particles within them, including electrons and protons, are *organized patterns of energy* which only *appear* to be solid matter.

Matter, the foundation of classical physics, is like a magician's illusion; it is not at all what it seems to be. The first thing to appreciate about the illusory nature of matter is that atoms are 99.999999999% empty space. The space between the orbiting electrons of an atom and its nucleus is proportionally enormous. If an atomic nucleus were to be drawn on paper as a one-inch dot, an electron orbiting the one-inch nucleus to be in proper scale would have to be drawn over a mile away.

The Physics of Miraculous Healing

There is an old saying: if you eliminate all the space in your body what is left would fit on the head of a pin. Why then doesn't our body mesh into other objects? Why doesn't it sink into the ground? The answer is that electrons, orbiting an atom's nucleus at speeds which are a significant fraction of the speed of light, create an impenetrable shell. Because of the high speed of their motion, and the tiny circumference of their orbit, in the time it takes to read this sentence a single electron will have circled an atom's nucleus *trillions* of times.

When the impenetrable electron shell of one atom comes in contact with another atom's impenetrable electron shell, the two atoms will most often repel each other. We don't sink into the floor because uncountable numbers of atoms in our feet are repelling uncountable numbers of atoms in the floor; uncountable numbers of atoms in the floor are repelling uncountable numbers of atoms in our feet; and the combined repelling force is far greater than the force of gravity trying to push our body into the floor.

The second thing to appreciate about the illusion of matter is that all the subatomic particles that make up the *nucleus* around which the electrons are orbiting are themselves nothing but energy. Countless experiments conducted in what used to be colorfully described as atom-smashers—the latest versions of which are called particle colliders, such as the Large Hadron Collider (LHC) in Switzerland—have failed to find any irreducibly small bits of solid matter in the nucleus. Instead, the nucleus of every atom has been revealed to be a dynamic balance of interacting organized patterns of energy.

The LHC accelerates two streams of protons to nearly the speed of light. Then, like orchestrating a head-on collision of two trains on the same track, the two proton streams are redirected to collide. When the two streams collide, the protons explode into a cloud of disorganized energy. Trillionths of a second after the explosion, the disorganized energy begins to reorganize into the patterns of specific particles: first into patterns that are known as exotic particles, highly unstable patterns that last only instants, that then combine and recombine until they once again become stable particle-patterns.

Although the cloud of disorganized energy almost instantly reorganizes into stable particle-patterns—*it does not necessarily reorganize into the same particle-patterns that the energy existed in before the collision.* Moreover, the extremely high energy imparted to the protons to accelerate them to nearly the speed of light *itself becomes part of the cloud of disorganized energy* that, after the collision, organizes into *additional* particle-patterns. In other words, colliders like the LHC actually create *new* particles.

The primary relevance of all the above to extraordinarily rapid, miraculous healing is that energy can assume any particle-pattern and thus can behave like any particle—and, significantly, can change its particle-pattern nearly *instantly*. From this perspective we can understand that the particle-patterns of energy in Barbara Cummiskey's body that had been organized into trillions of *unhealthy* cells, in a few miraculous moments reorganized into trillions of *healthy* cells.

Wave-Particle Duality and the Observer Effect

Even more mind-boggling than that matter is an illusion is the discovery known as *wave-particle duality*. Energy organized in particle-patterns, thus behaving as matter, can, under certain conditions, reorganize as *invisible waves of energy*. Similarly, energy organized as invisible waves of energy, such as sunlight, can, under certain conditions, reorganize as particle-patterns known as photons. All energy, whether behaving as particles or behaving as energy-waves, has the Jekyll-Hyde ability to switch back and forth.

The discovery of wave-particle duality was followed by a discovery even more confounding to common sense: energy organizes into particle-patterns, and thus behaves like matter, *only when observed by an intelligent observer.*

The Physics of Miraculous Healing

If you are unfamiliar with quantum physics, what I just stated probably makes no sense at all—nor did it to the physicists of the 1920s. The discovery of wave-particle duality and the observer effect left physicists feeling they had joined Alice at the Mad Hatter's tea party.

The best way I know to describe the discovery, and to convey just how counterintuitive it is, is to walk you through an oft-repeated series of experiments, the results of which never fail to leave people bemusedly shaking their heads.

These experiments are commonly known as double-slit experiments. Light's wave-like behavior can be demonstrated by shining a single beam of light through two side-by-side vertical slits in a barrier (see figure 1), thus creating two new side-by-side beams of light. The two new side-by-side beams of light fan out and interfere with each other like water waves in a pond.

When water-wave troughs meet, they form a deeper trough. When water-wave crests meet, they form a higher crest. When troughs meet crests, they cancel each other out in proportion to their respective depths or heights. The overall result of water-waves intersecting is a regular pattern of increased peaks and troughs alternating with decreased peaks and troughs. This regular pattern, known as an interference pattern, visible on the detector in figure 1 as alternating bands of light and dark, confirms that light behaves as a wave.

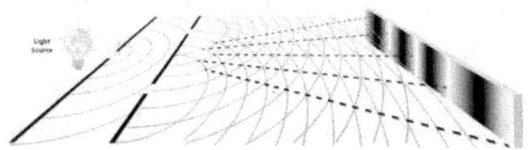

Figure 1: Light shows its wavelike nature when it passes through the double slits and forms two new beams of light, which then interfere with each other in the same way as water waves. On the far right of the image you can see the characteristic interference pattern that forms on a detector. The brighter bands show where two wave crests meet and create a higher crest or two

The Physics of Miraculous Healing

troughs meet and form a deeper trough. The darker bands show where crests meet troughs and partially or fully cancel each other out.

Physicists, trying to understand the nature of light more fully, devised another double-slit experiment. Instead of shining a light continuously through the two slits, they developed a way to send photons, light's particle form, one at a time through the slits. The pattern physicists expected to see on the detector was like the pattern bullets would make when fired from a gun into a target (figure 2).

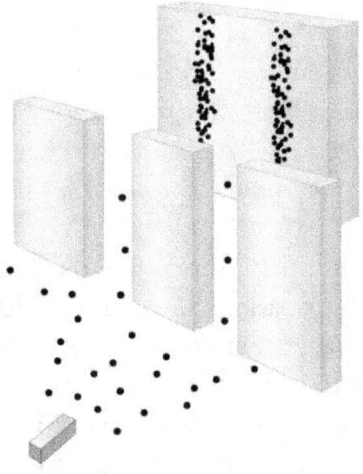

Figure 2: What physicists expected to see on the detector—two bands of photon impacts comparable to bullets hitting a target.

Imagine the experimenters' astonishment when, even though only one photon was released at a time, each photon still behaved as if it were part of a wave interfering with another wave (figure 3). Impossible as such behavior seems it has been confirmed in experiments again and again.

The Physics of Miraculous Healing

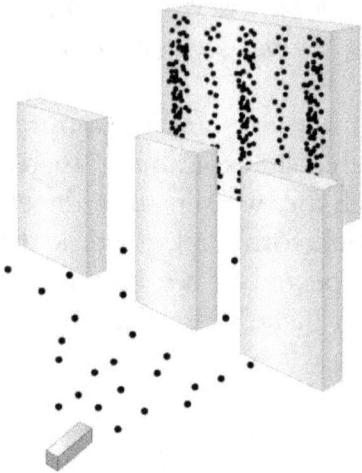

Figure 3: What was actually seen in the experiments, even though the photons were sent one at a time through the slits, was the same interference pattern as one sees in figure 1—a little rougher than the interference pattern created by a continuous light source, but unmistakably the same pattern.

Collectively scratching their heads, physicists tried to understand how this paradoxical result could occur. Eventually they conducted another experiment: a measuring device was placed by the slits to detect which slit an individual photon traveled through. (The measuring device does not interfere in any way with the passage of the photons through the slits.) Now try to imagine the experimenters' even deeper astonishment: once the measuring device was added to the experiment, the photons passed through the slits and hit the detector like bullets fired from a gun (figure 4).

The Physics of Miraculous Healing

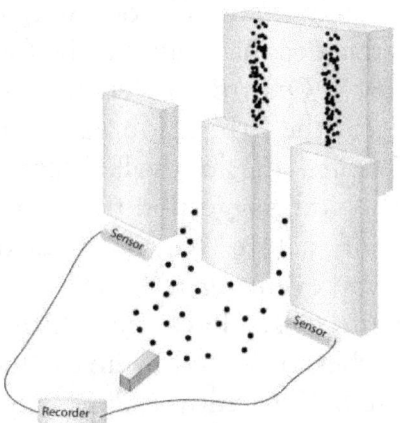

Figure 4: Once the experiment was set up to measure which slit individual photons were passing through, the photons behaved like particles and created the pattern on the detector one would expect of little bits of matter.

Why?! Why did the photons behave differently? Nothing had changed! The *only* difference in the two experimental setups was that the passage of the photons through the slits had been *measured*.

Physicists have subsequently performed this same experiment, always with the same result, using atoms and molecules instead of photons. They have found that, when they are not measured as they pass through the slits, atoms and molecules behave like waves of energy, but when they are measured as they pass through the slits, they behave like particles.

Welcome to quantum weirdness.

Physicists call this the *measurement effect,* but because there needs to be an intelligent observer who performs the process of measurement the phenomenon began also to be known as the *intelligent observer effect.* Niels Bohr—considered the father of quantum physics and whose reputation as a scientist is only slightly less lofty than Einstein's—was among the first to conclude from such experiments that energy only behaves like matter when we observe it.

This conclusion didn't, and still doesn't, sit well with many physicists. It turns the idea that matter is the foundation of reality upside down. In 1987, Oxford University's Dr. David Deutsch wrote in an article for the British Journal for the Philosophy of Science that, "Despite the unrivalled empirical success of quantum theory, the very suggestion that it may be literally true as a description of nature is still greeted with cynicism, incomprehension, and even anger."[1]

Though many physicists have tried, Bohr's assertion that matter exists only when observed by an intelligent observer has never been disproved. As recently as 2018, a Scientific American article entitled, *"Coming to Grips with the Implications of Quantum Mechanics,"* describes the many attempts to disprove the need for an intelligent observer—and explains why all those attempts have failed.[2]

Although many physicists don't like it—and I can attest that I am often challenged by physicists exasperated with me for putting it forward as a confirmed effect—the need for an intelligent observer to make energy behave like matter remains demonstrably true. *Why* it happens is a subject of much debate; but *that* it happens isn't. As quantum physicist Amit Goswami simply and uncompromisingly puts it, "There is no object…without a conscious subject looking at it."[3]

Energy-Wave Behavior in the Body

Despite double-slit experiments revealing that an intelligent observer causes energy to organize into particle-patterns and thus behave like matter, and that without an intelligent observer the energy will behave as energy-waves, most physicists nonetheless assume that the energy that makes up all the *unobserved* atoms and molecules *inside* material objects will also behave like matter. They make this assumption because they believe that all the energies, whether on the surface or within an observed material object, are part of an *interconnected observed system*—observe one interconnected atom and you observe them

The Physics of Miraculous Healing

all. Most physicists assume, therefore, that all the energy that makes up matter will *always* behave like matter unless it is put into a highly controlled, *artificially* created environment, such as those created for double-slit experiments.

This assumption was believed to be especially true in what has been often described as the *warm, wet conditions* found inside the human body. Growing numbers of discoveries indicate, however, that *some* of the energy that makes up the human body does, in fact, behave as energy-waves even as the energy in other parts of the body behaves as matter.

These recent discoveries are based on the detection of what are known as *coherent* energy-waves in the human body. Coherent energy-waves are different from the electromagnetic energy waves that radiate out from a source simultaneously in every direction. Coherent energy waves are more like the laser light-waves that all go in a single direction. Further, coherent energy waves vibrate at the same frequency, in phase, and in alignment—like rowers in a boat rowing at precisely the same speed (frequency), beginning and ending their strokes at precisely the same moment (in phase), and sitting in precisely the same physical positions (in alignment).

The detection of coherent energy-waves in the body is highly significant because when energy behaves in the same way as atoms or molecules, it behaves *decoherently*, each atom or molecule vibrating at its own frequency, out of phase and out of alignment with all the other atoms and molecules around it. Thus, finding evidence of coherent energy-waves in the body means that at least *some* of the atoms and molecules in the body have made the Jekyll-Hyde switch to behave as energy-waves.

In the 1970s, researchers at the University of Marburg in Germany, led by Fritz-Albert Popp, scanned the human body to measure a well-documented phenomenon, known as biophotons—the emission of photons from living organisms. Popp's team scanned the human body to measure not just the *presence* of biophotons but the *frequencies* of the biophotons emitted. They expected to find, based on the then current assumptions in physics, that the timing and frequency of *every* biophoton emission would be random. They found instead that nearly all biophoton emissions were coherent—in the same frequency, phase, and alignment—an effect that could only be possible if the atoms inside the body from which the biophotons were emitted were behaving as coherent energy-waves.[4]

Based on many experiments looking for coherent energy-waves in the brain, in 2007, Gregory S. Engel, Professor in Chemistry at The University of Chicago wrote that "all arguments concerning the brain being "too warm and wet" have been dispelled, as multiple "warm and wet" quantum processes have been discovered."[5]

The Missing Speed

Scientists working in the newly emerging field of quantum biology, in attempting to better understand how chlorophyll molecules harvest the energy of the sun, discovered that during the process of photosynthesis, thousands of chlorophyll molecules in a leaf become a single coherent energy-wave.[6] When the thousands of chlorophyll molecules become coherent energy-waves, they become a *resistance-free superconductor for the transfer of the sun's energy*—far faster and far more efficient at capturing and transferring the sun's energy than manmade systems such as solar panels.

The increased speed and efficiency of a leaf's coherent chlorophyll-superconductor suggests that the top speed of the production of proteins, ATP molecules, or any other life-process, could be increased if the atoms and molecules involved made the Jekyll-Hyde switch to behaving as coherent energy-waves. This increased speed could bridge the gap between the estimates of how many proteins need to be produced each day to support a healthy adult body and the estimates of how fast the molecular-machines in our cells, such as ribosomes and mitochondria, can realistically produce proteins and ATP.

The Physics of Miraculous Healing

Because the energy that makes up the body can behave both coherently and decoherently—as energy-waves or as atoms and molecules—the body can be compared to a hybrid-electric car. A hybrid-electric car has both an internal combustion engine and an electric motor. Some hybrid-electric cars will use both the slower internal combustion engine and the faster electric motor simultaneously to achieve the car's highest speed. Similarly, the body can conduct life-processes simultaneously using its slower decoherent molecular-machines made of atoms and molecules and its faster coherent energy-waves to achieve the body's highest pace of executing life-processes.

The coherent chlorophyll-superconductor also suggests that the energy that makes up living organisms can shift from decoherent to coherent behavior *naturally*, without artificial inducement, as a routine option for executing life-processes. In the next chapter we will explore the natural cause and source of coherent behavior. Expect to be surprised.

CHAPTER 3—The Body Extends into Another Realm

Physicists know that coherent energy-waves exist—but they also know, paradoxically, that coherent energy-waves *cannot exist in the physical world*. The physical world behaves according to the laws of classical physics—and the laws of classical physics don't support the behavior of coherent energy-waves. This paradox led physicists to conclude that there must be another realm that is separate from, but inextricably connected to, our familiar physical world, a separate realm which behaves according to another set of laws. This separate realm became known as *nonlocality*.

Nonlocality

As early as the 1920s, physicists began to refer to behaviors such as coherent energy-waves and the observer effect as *nonlocal* behaviors, in contrast to the more familiar *local* behaviors we experience in our everyday physical world. In our local physical world, for example, electromagnetic energy, such as visible light, rapidly weakens as it moves away from its source because light waves radiate outward into space in all directions. The farther from the source, the more dispersed the light rays become; the more dispersed they become, the weaker they are at any given point away from the point of origin.

The Physics of Miraculous Healing

Nonlocal coherent energy-waves, on the other hand, never weaken.

That coherent energy-waves never weaken, and other evidence of nonlocal behaviors such as quantum entanglement, have led physicists to understand the counterintuitive nature of this other reality.

Two-Dimensional

Nonlocality is two-dimensional, unlike our more familiar three-dimensional physical world. Nonlocality's two-dimensionality is the fundamental cause of many of its behaviors.

Spaceless

Because there are only two dimensions in nonlocality, there is *no space*; there must be three-dimensions for space to exist. In nonlocality, coherent energy-waves never weaken, because there is no space in which they can disperse.

Matterless

Because energy can only behave like matter where there is three-dimensional space, in nonlocality *there is no matter*. In nonlocality, decoherent matter simply can't exist.

Timeless

Because there is no space, in nonlocality *there is no time*. In nonlocality, cause and effect occur simultaneously; there is no time delay caused by matter or energy traveling through space.

Pure Energy

Because energy needs only two dimensions in which to vibrate, spaceless nonlocality consists purely of energy.

One Interconnected Whole

Because there is no space, matter, or time, pure-energy nonlocality is one interconnected whole. In nonlocality, everything is entangled.

Interpenetrating

Not only is there no space in nonlocality, there is no space *between* nonlocality and any point in the local physical universe: Nonlocality's energy *interpenetrates our physical universe everywhere*.

The Physics of Miraculous Healing

Although nonlocality sounds as if it must be somewhere else, it's not—it's right here—interpenetratingly present.

The Body is Both Local and Nonlocal

We saw in the last chapter that the energy that makes up the body can behave in two different ways—as decoherent particles or as coherent energy-waves. When we add nonlocality to that picture, we see that the energy that makes up the body has two realities in which it exists. The energy that makes up the body is constantly dancing out of locality into nonlocality and back again; out of decoherent particles into coherent energy-waves and back again; out of unintegrated space, matter, and time into one integrated whole and back again.

> We must liberate man from the [physical]…in which, since the renaissance, he has been imprisoned. We now know that we…extend outside the physical continuum…. In time, as well as in space, the individual stretches out beyond the frontiers of his body…. He also belongs to another world.—Dr. Alexis Carrel, Nobel Prize winner[1]

Our Local Universe is a Tiny Part of the Cosmos

Nonlocality is far more than a weird abstraction necessary to account for otherwise unexplainable quantum effects. Nonlocality, according to string theory, a particular branch of quantum physics, is home to the vast majority of energy in the cosmos, and it is upon the energy in nonlocality that the entire local physical universe depends for its existence.

Over the span of the twentieth and now the twenty-first century, many branches of physics have added brush strokes to a picture of an astonishingly vast and predominantly nonmaterial cosmos, a cosmos in which our already mind-bendingly enormous physical universe is only a self-contained, three-dimensional "bubble" within a virtually infinite nonlocal two-dimensional "ocean" of energy.

The Physics of Miraculous Healing

It's necessary to paint this picture of the cosmos to explain a fundamental mystery. Quantum physics is extremely accurate. It can predict "real-world" outcomes of physical systems, such as the energy output of nuclear power plants, to the highest degree of accuracy. Yet quantum physics' equations, in order to work, must assume that there is vastly more energy present in the fabric of the universe than has ever been measured with physical instruments—10^{122} times more! Unless that colossally greater amount of energy is somehow always present, quantum physics simply doesn't add up. Because the equations of quantum physics do add up, and extremely well at that, physicists have no doubt that the missing energy must be *somewhere*, even if it can't be measured with physical instruments.

String theory, which made its debut in the mid-twentieth century, was born in part out of the need to account for this unmeasurable energy. String theory posits that there exists a vast number of ultra-tiny, two-dimensional rings and strings of coherent energy-waves that vibrate at wavelengths far, far smaller than those measurable with our most sensitive physical instruments. These rings and strings are thought to be a *billion* times smaller than the nucleus of an atom. String theory posits that *everything* in our local physical universe is born of these two-dimensional infinitesimally small rings and strings of vibrating energy—giving rise to all matter and all measurable energy—and even space itself.

Enter M-theory.

M-theory, the currently most accepted version of string theory, posits two competing views of how, and in a sense, *where* those nonlocal rings and strings exist: one view has them existing in *compactified dimensions* and another has them existing in *large extra dimensions*.

The compactified-dimensions view posits that there are many more dimensions compacted into the three dimensions of space. Proponents of this view describe extra dimensions being "wrapped up" or "curled up" on themselves. The compactified-

The Physics of Miraculous Healing

dimensions view supports a vision of reality in which the rings and strings of missing energy are contained *within* the universe.

The large-extra-dimensions view posits that there are many more dimensions *beyond* the physical universe. Proponents of this view describe a vast nonlocal reality composed solely of energy. They refer to this vast pure-energy nonlocal reality as the *bulk*, a name which arose from the idea that it contains the "bulk of reality." In the large-extra-dimensions view the bulk has a layered structure. Each layer is a distinct large extra dimension called a *brane*. The word brane is a contraction of the word membrane and is used to suggest a barrier or boundary that divides or encloses, keeping the contents of one region separate from other regions.

In the large-extra-dimensions view, each brane contains energies vibrating within a discrete range of frequencies different from those of all other branes; the result is a hierarchy of branes beginning with the brane with the highest frequencies of energies and descending brane-layer by brane-layer to the brane with the lowest frequencies of energy. Depending on the mathematical assumptions M-theorists make, the number of two-dimensional branes that exist in the bulk varies from *brane world scenario* to *brane world scenario*.

Support for Brane World Scenarios

While there is mathematical support within string theory and M-theory for either compactified dimensions or brane worlds, my own view is that brane worlds are a better description of reality. Why? As I wrote in the introduction, some disciplines on the frontier of physics provide a bridge between science and spirituality without any loss of scientific rigor. In this specific case, the theory of multiple branes making up the bulk—a description of reality as essentially infinite, existing beyond the physical universe, containing only high-frequency vibrating energy, and having a layer-like structure—matches astonishingly well the descriptions of the *heavens*, or luminous *astral regions*, given by saints, sages, and near-death experiencers.

> Heaven is a world much like our own except there is no time nor space as we think of them here. Heaven exists in a higher dimension of energy. The higher realms are a world of inexpressible beauty.—Nora Spurgin, near-death experiencer and researcher[2]

> Time as I had known it came to a halt; past, present, and future were somehow fused together for me in the timeless unity of life. I learned that all the physical rules for human life were nothing when compared to this unitive reality.—George Rodonaia, near-death experiencer[3]

The literature of those who've had near-death experiences and the transcendent experiences of the spiritually awakened are full of such descriptions. The heavens or astral regions are glowingly and consistently described as surpassingly beautiful, surpassingly finer versions of the world we know. Time does not flow as we experience it. Movement is not governed by Newton's laws of motion or by Einstein's speed of light.

> The higher realms are a world of inexpressible beauty. They are realms of endless possibilities for creativity and full realization of self; and they are where the love of God is like the air we breathe.—Nora Spurgin, near-death experiencer and researcher[4]

> [Heaven] is filled with some sort of beautiful light…people…flowers…angels…. All is filled with some indescribable joy. Heaven…has a brilliant light which does not leave it.—Vicka Ivankovic-Mijatovic, one of the six children who experienced the Visions of Mary in Medjugorje, Bosnia Herzegovina[5]

> The [heavenly] astral kingdom is a realm of rainbow-hued light. Astral land, seas, skies, gardens, beings, the manifestation of day and night—all are made of variegated vibrations of light. Oceans heave with

The Physics of Miraculous Healing

opalescent azure, green, silver, gold, red, yellow, and aquamarine. Diamond-bright waves dance in a perpetual rhythm of beauty.—Paramhansa Yogananda, yoga master[6]

Heaven is far more subtle and mutable than our physical existence, yet those who experience it say it feels unquestionably real—in fact, *much more* real than our physical world. C. G. Jung (1875–1961) wrote in his autobiographical *Memories, Dreams, Reflections* descriptions of a near-death experience he had in 1944 while in a hospital as the result of a heart attack. During his near death he experienced profound freedom and ecstasy. For several weeks after his initial experience, while still in hospital convalescence, he had blissfully transcendent visions during the night and difficulty reintegrating with his physical body during the day:

> It is impossible to convey the beauty and intensity of emotion during those visions. They were the most tremendous things I have ever experienced. And what a contrast the day was: I was tormented and on edge; everything irritated me; everything was too material, too crude and clumsy, terribly limited both spatially and spiritually. It was all an imprisonment, for reasons impossible to divine, and yet it had a kind of hypnotic power, a cogency, as if it were reality itself, for all that I had clearly perceived its emptiness. Although my belief in the world returned to me, I have never entirely freed myself of the impression that…this life is a segment of existence which is enacted in a three-dimensional box-like universe especially set up for it.[7]

Not only do descriptions of the qualities of two-dimensional branes match descriptions of the heavens, descriptions of the branes' layered structure matches traditions of multiple layers, levels, or realms in heaven.

In the Christian tradition we find many biblical references to multiple heavens:

The Physics of Miraculous Healing

> I know a man in Christ who fourteen years ago was caught up to the third heaven. Whether it was in the body or out of the body I do not know.—2 Cor. 12:2-4
>
> But who is able to build a temple for him, since the heavens, even the highest heavens, cannot contain him?—2 Chron. 2:6

In Judaism there is a long tradition of mysticism contained in the teachings of the Kabbalah. The transcendent experiences described by Kabbalah practitioners include visits to ten subtle angelic realms which exist within ten emanations of Light that continuously create both the physical realm and a chain of higher realms. The ten emanations of Light are known collectively as *Sephirot*. Each emanation of light is described as being progressively more refined, higher, and more subtle than the one below.

One of the highest holy days of the Muslim calendar, *Lailat al Mi'raj*, celebrates Mohammed's journey through seven heavens, as described in the Hadith. Mohammed is taken, while his body sleeps, through seven increasingly more exalted realms, each with its own qualities and purpose.

The Buddhists, including Zen and Tibetan Buddhists, similarly hold a belief in a hierarchy of realms. Some traditions have ten realms—our physical realm, plus many more heavenly realms through which souls move between incarnations as they work out their karma. Hinduism's heavenly descriptions contain a hierarchy of seven realms or *lokas*, each more subtle than the last, beginning with *Bhuva Loka*, the physical world, and ending with *Satya Loka*, the highest heaven.

Such conceptions of the heavens are also confirmed by near-death experiencers:

> There are many different Heavens.... They are stacked one atop the other like pancakes and scattered all throughout God's super Universe.—Christian Andreason, near-death experiencer[8]

The Physics of Miraculous Healing

That such an obvious and direct similarity exists between M-theory's branes and brane worlds and the conceptions of the heavens and astral worlds found in all experiential spiritual teachings, as well as in most of the world's religions, inclines me to believe that M-theory's almost purely mathematical deduction of large extra nonlocal dimensions is going in the right direction. M-theorists are likely to be aghast that I compare their brane worlds to the heavens, but there can be only one reality. Science explores the one reality through indirect experimentation; saints and sages explore the one reality through direct experience.

There is a compelling consistency to spiritual experience that one begins to appreciate the more one studies the lives and teachings of saints and sages as well as the stirring descriptions of near-death experiencers. Are we to believe that the consistent experiences described by saints and sages through several millennia are all delusional, or worse, fraudulent? That the men and women who have inspired the fulfilling moral behavior and thrilling spiritual vision in billions of people just made it up?

We have been conditioned by matter-centered biology to believe that everything it is *possible* to experience must arise from local matter. Although scientists have not yet been able to explain how consciousness, emotion, or thought *do* arise from local neural interactions in the brain, many people are convinced that it is only a matter of time before the biological mechanisms of consciousness and subjective experience will become clear. This prevalent belief leads people simply to assume that their own subjective experiences—from love to inspiration to transcendence—are nothing more than local electrochemical neural phenomena taking place in their brain.

It is the widely held assumption that all our experiences must be local physical phenomena that keeps most people from realizing that *most* of their own experiences are nonlocal energetic phenomena. Once you appreciate the qualities of nonlocality, you can appreciate that consciousness, emotion, and thought behave as nonlocal phenomena—not subject to local laws of space and time; unaffected by distance; not weakened or dissipated by time.

Experiential spiritual teachings such as yoga, Sufism, tai chi, Zen Buddhism, Daoism, the Jewish Kabbalah, and Christian mysticism include core practices, particularly meditation, through which the individual can transcend the limited local awareness provided by our senses and directly experience more subtle nonlocal realities. Advanced practitioners develop into saints, sages, and mystics because directly experiencing themselves as part of nonlocal reality is potently transformative.

Additionally, experiential spiritual teachings are confirmed by many near-death experiencers. Ironic as it is that matter-centered medicine's highly effective trauma care can enable matter-transcending personal experience, the fact remains that millions of people have described transcendent, powerfully life-changing, spiritually uplifting experiences that occurred during trauma-care—experiences that echo many of the transcendent experiences described by saints, sages, and mystics.

The main barrier to finding common ground between experimental scientific discovery and experiential spiritual discovery has been the predominant view of scientists that all that is real is a result of the local laws of matter and electromagnetic energy, and that human experience must be, therefore, purely material and confined to the physical universe. In contrast, M-theory's brane worlds provide solid scientific credibility for the existence of a realm that lies beyond the physical universe, a realm which is governed by nonlocal laws that supersede local laws of matter and electromagnetic energy, a realm upon which our local physical universe depends for its very existence, and which suggests that, to again quote Dr. Alexis Carrel, "the individual stretches out beyond the frontiers of his body…. He also belongs to another world."[9]

The Physics of Miraculous Healing

CHAPTER 4—The Body is Holographic

Why Does Matter Take a Specific Form?

One of the first questions the discovery of the intelligent observer effect led physicists to ask was what causes the energy that makes up matter to behave as a specific type of atom when it *is* observed? When the energy is not observed, when it is behaving as coherent energy-waves, does it invisibly maintain a predetermined atomic form? Or is there no predetermined form at all? Is the specific atomic form energy takes when observed a random accident?

The theory that the specific atomic form energy takes when observed is a random accident, a widely held view among physicists then and now, prompted Einstein's most famous saying: "God does not play dice." He felt that *hidden properties* which would predetermine atomic form *must* exist even while energy is behaving as coherent energy-waves, thus ensuring that when the energy making up atoms *is* observed, it would take on a specific predetermined form and no other. But, alas, as of 1955, the year of Einstein's death, no explanation for hidden properties had been found.

Not long after Einstein's passing, however, physicist David Bohm, a well-regarded early pioneer of quantum physics with a long list of notable discoveries to his credit, came up with a new explanation—that hidden properties did predetermine atomic form but that they hadn't been found because they exist in nonlocality—thus putting them beyond our ability to detect or measure. He went on to develop a version of quantum mechanics, known as *Bohmian mechanics*, that makes a strong mathematical case for the existence of nonlocal hidden properties based on what has become known in physics as the *holographic principle*.

The Holographic Principle

Holograms are two-dimensional. *Holographic projections* are three-dimensional. Holographic images are stored in *flat*, two-dimensional, media. When laser-light interacts with the flat, two-dimensional media, however, it creates a three-dimensional holographic projection. A holographic projection does not simply *appear* to be three-dimensional, it *is*. Walk around a holographic projection and you will see different sides of a three-dimensional object—all generated from two-dimensional media.

Bohm saw not only conceptual, but mathematical similarities between terrestrial holography and the interactions between local and nonlocal energy. He theorized that, in nonlocality, precisely organized two-dimensional coherent energy-waves act as a hologram, from which local three-dimensional atoms and molecules are holographically projected. Put another way, Bohm recognized that the reason energy, when observed, behaves as *specific* three-dimensional local atoms and molecules is that the guiding template determining the form of those atoms and molecules preexists as a *specific* two-dimensional nonlocal hologram.

In part because of Bohm's work, other disciplines of physics eventually embraced the holographic principle, most notably, M-theory. M-theorists have developed equations that indicate that *the entire three-dimensional physical universe is a holographic projection.*

> The three-dimensional world of ordinary experience—
> —the universe filled with galaxies, stars, planets, houses, boulders, and people—is [contained in] a hologram, an

> image of reality coded on a…two-dimensional surface.—Dr. Leonard Susskind, Stanford professor and leading M-theorist[1]

Are you astonished by this quote? I was. Not because I find it difficult to believe, but because Susskind, as respected a physicist as you will find, is straight forwardly and unambiguously saying that not only is the material universe a holographic projection but so are the "people" in it! He is stating, unequivocally, that our physical bodies, as well as everything else in the physical universe, are three-dimensional holographic projections that come from a holographic "image of reality coded on a…two-dimensional surface."

Further Experiential Support for M-Theory

Although astonished by Susskind's assertion I did not find it difficult to believe. His description of the holographic principle—that the holographic information that determines the form of the entire physical universe doesn't exist in the physical universe itself but in a nonlocal two-dimensional hologram—matches the description given by saints, sages, and near-death experiencers. They maintain that it is the *heavens* that determine the form of the physical universe and everything in it—including our physical bodies.

The brilliant polymath and Christian mystic, Emanuel Swedenborg (1688–1772), began his life in Sweden as a scientist and inventor. Widely acknowledged as a scientific genius, he pioneered many new directions in geometry, chemistry, metallurgy, anatomy, and physiology. At age fifty-two, he turned his inquisitive mind to more subtle realities. For almost thirty years, his inner researches led to numerous personal transcendent experiences. One finding was that the heavens provide a template for the natural world; he refers to the connection between heaven and earth as a "correspondence":

> In a word, absolutely everything in nature, from the smallest to the greatest, is a correspondence. The reason

correspondences occur is that the natural world, including everything in it, arises and is sustained from the spiritual world, and both worlds come from the Divine.²

Swedenborg is not alone in having witnessed such a correspondence:

> The blueprints of everything in the physical universe have been astrally conceived—all the forms and forces in nature, including the complex human body, have been first produced in that realm where God's causal ideations are made visible in forms of heavenly light and vibratory energy.—Paramhansa Yogananda, yoga master³

> Everything was created of spirit matter before it was created physically—solar systems, suns, moons, stars, planets, life upon the planets, mountains, rivers, seas, etc. I saw this process, and then, to further understand it, I was told . . . that the spirit creation could be compared to one of our photographic prints; the spirit creation would be like a sharp, brilliant print, and the Earth would be like its dark negative. This Earth is only a shadow of the beauty and glory of its spirit creation.—Betty J. Eadie, *Embraced by the Light*⁴

The Subtle Energy Body

The holographic principle described by M-theory also supports and is supported by another basic teaching from the traditions of experiential spirituality: that each one of us has a *subtle energy body*, variously called *astral body*, *spirit body*, *light body*, or *etheric body*, and that it is the subtle energy body that creates, maintains, and determines, *moment by moment*, every aspect of our physical body.

There are individuals, often called psychics, clairvoyants, or intuitives, who can "see" the subtle energy body. They perceive the energy body as a multicolored aura that surrounds and suffuses the physical body. Any change in a person's feelings, thoughts, and health is immediately apparent in the subtle energy body: colors move and change, colors become clearer or muddier, areas of the aura become brighter or dimmer, or the overall aura may expand or contract. Auras, also described as halos, are frequently depicted in religious paintings and sculptures. Every spiritual tradition describes saints and sages as being surrounded by a holy, otherworldly light.

> I can tell you that anything that happens in the physical body will happen in the pattern of the energy fields first.—Barbara Brennan, healer, author of *Hands of Light*[5]

> Clairvoyants can see flashes of colour, constantly changing, in the aura that surrounds every person: each thought, each feeling, thus translating itself in the astral world, visible to the astral sight.—Annie Besant, clairvoyant, Theosophical Society president[6]

Life After Death

According to the direct experience of saints, sages, and near-death experiencers, when we die, our awareness switches from awareness of the world around us and our physical body to awareness of the heavens and our subtle energy body. We don't really die; we simply no longer have a physical body of which we can be aware. Our memories, emotions, and thoughts live on where they have always been, in our already existing, better, finer, look-alike subtle energy body—look-alike because it has all along been the hologram for the holographic projection that is the physical body.

> Never before had I considered that there might be such things as coexistent realities. Never had I imagined that there might be concurrent realms. I realized that in life, death is merely the other side of a threshold over which I could not "normally" see. So, too, in death, life and the land of the "living" were on the other side of a very thin veil.—Lynnclaire Dennis, near-death experiencer[7]

The Physics of Miraculous Healing

> Using radio as an analogy, [death] is comparable to having lived all your life at a certain radio frequency when all of a sudden someone or something comes along and flips the dial. You shift frequencies in dying. You switch over to life on another wavelength. You don't die when you die. You shift your consciousness and speed of vibration. That's all death is . . . a shift.—P. M. H. Atwater, near-death researcher and experiencer[8]
>
> What we consider the here and now, this world, it is actually just the material level that is comprehensible [to the senses]. The beyond is an infinite reality that is much bigger. Which this world is rooted in. In this way, our lives in this plane of existence are encompassed, surrounded, by the afterworld already. . . . The body dies but the spiritual quantum field continues. In this way, I am immortal.—Dr. Hans-Peter Dürr, former head of the Max Planck Institute for Physics, Munich[9]

From near-death experiencers we also learn that their experience of themselves while "dead" was very similar to their experience of themselves while living: they could recall memories of their life before they died; they thought and reasoned in the same way, although more clearly; they felt emotions in the same way, although their primary feeling was of joyful freedom; and they were clearly, even exceptionally aware, often remarking after becoming once again conscious of their physical body, that their experience had been more real than the one to which they returned.

> Almost all people who arrive [in heaven] from this world are as astonished as they can be to find that they are alive and that they are just as human as ever.—Emanuel Swedenborg, Christian mystic[10]

I find the parallels between physics and spirituality revealed by these concepts—holograms and holographic projections and astral bodies and physical bodies—to be both inspiring and enlightening. On a large scale they reveal the mechanisms of creation; the local matter and energy of the universe is completely dependent on nonlocal holographic information. On a small scale they reveal the mechanisms of the body; the local matter and energy that make up the physical body are completely dependent on nonlocal holographic information. As quoted above, "The blueprints of everything in the physical universe...including the complex human body, have been first produced in that realm where God's causal ideations are made visible in forms of heavenly light and vibratory energy."[11]

How the Holographic Principle Applies to Health and Healing

No Speed Limit—No Change Limit

It is the holographic nature of the body that enables extraordinarily rapid, even instantaneous, physical change. In nonlocality there is no time; cause and effect are simultaneous. Whatever the rate and extent of change in the patterns of coherent energy-waves of the hologram-subtle energy body, that same rate and extent of change will manifest in the physical body—whether the rate of change is slow, fast, or instantaneous, and whether a few atoms or trillions of cells are changed.

No Condition or Disease is Incurable

It is true that some conditions or diseases can't be cured by drugs or surgery because the local biochemical laws that govern drugs and surgery are *limited* to affecting only the local three-dimensional holographic projection, making drugs and surgery subject to the relatively slow and mechanistic ways in which biochemical laws work. Nonlocal influences, on the other hand, that directly affect the hologram-subtle energy body—the source of the holographic projection itself—aren't slow, mechanistic, or limited. Nonlocal influences instantly and directly change the hologram—which in turn instantly and directly changes the holographic projection that is the physical body.

The Physics of Miraculous Healing

Coordination of Life-Processes

The holographic nature of the body also enables the coordination of the physical body's quadrillions of molecular processes occurring every second across its forty to sixty trillion cells—sextillion times a day the right protein is produced at the right time. Although DNA contains no programming and the brain and nervous system aren't fast enough or vast enough to coordinate such a stupendous volume of life-processes, that coordination can take place within our hologram-subtle energy body *instantaneously and continuously* in timeless nonlocality. It helps to think of your hologram-subtle energy body not as a static template but as a movie film that projects a three-dimensional movie—a living movie film, if you will, that contains all the information required to direct the holographic projection, moment-by-moment, of every atom and molecule in the physical body.

CHAPTER 5—The Body is Intelligently Guided

The holographic dynamic enables the astonishing pace of intra-cellular life processes, extraordinarily rapid physical change, and the continuous coordination of the body's quadrillions-per-second life-processes. But there remains an important question: If the subtle energy body coordinates all life-processes occurring in the physical body by acting as a film-like template for the dynamic holographic process, what coordinates the film-like template itself?

Understandably awed by the astonishing complexity of living organisms, people tend to attribute it to Mother Nature, the Miracle of life, or simply Life. Many people intuitively believe that those capital letters are deserved, that a *higher Intelligence* must be at work to ensure the origin and continuation of biological life. Even more than most people, doctors, who have direct contact with patients in life and death situations, believe in higher Intelligence. Of 1,044 doctors surveyed by the University of Chicago in 2005, 76 percent said they believe in higher Intelligence.[1]

> [There is] a kind of superintelligence that exists in each of us, infinitely smarter and possessed of technical know-how far beyond our present understanding.—Dr. Bernie Siegel, author of *Love, Medicine, and Miracles*[2]

The Physics of Miraculous Healing

Many Scientists Believe in a Higher Intelligence

You might think, given the strong core of materialism in science, that most scientists would dismiss out of hand the concept of higher Intelligence. Interestingly, a Pew Research survey in 2009 found that 51 percent of scientists believed in God, a higher power, or *higher Intelligence,* and many notable scientists have said as much.

> You will hardly find one among the profounder sort of scientific minds without a peculiar religious feeling of his own. But it is different from the religion of the naive man. His religious feeling takes the form of a rapturous amazement at the harmony of natural law, which reveals an intelligence of such superiority that, compared with it, all the systematic thinking and acting of human beings is an utterly insignificant reflection.—Albert Einstein[3]

> [It] becomes sensible to think that the favorable properties of physics on which life depends are in every respect deliberate.... It is therefore almost inevitable that our own measure of intelligence must reflect...higher intelligences...even to the limit of God...such a theory is so obvious that one wonders why it is not widely accepted as being self-evident. The reasons are psychological rather than scientific.—Fred Hoyle, mathematician and astronomer[4]

> I have concluded that we are in a world made by rules created by an intelligence. To me it is clear that we exist in a plan which is governed by rules that were created, shaped by a universal intelligence and not by chance.—Michio Kaku, string theorist[5]

> All matter originates and exists only by virtue of a force which brings the particle of an atom to vibration and holds this most minute solar system of the atom together. We must assume behind this force the existence of a conscious and intelligent mind. This mind is the

matrix of all matter.—Max Planck, Nobel-prize winner in physics[6]

We are Players in a Cosmic Movie
Not only is the film-like template that is the subtle energy body Intelligently guided, M-theory's holographic principle offers the first scientific support for the belief in many experiential spiritual traditions that the entire universe is a continuously created, Intelligently guided, *cosmic movie*: the local three-dimensional physical universe is the projected movie and the nonlocal two-dimensional pure-energy hologram is the cosmic film. Our continuously changing local universe is the exact projection of its continuously changing Intelligently guided nonlocal hologram.

Using television as an analogy, the picture we enjoy seeing, the progression of the storyline with characters acting out a script, is but a trick of perception. Your mind connects the electron/dots into the picture images you think you see, while it totally ignores the true reality of what actually undergirds the operation. Existence is a lot like television. What exists, what really exists, can't be fathomed by how it appears to operate or what it seems to be.—P. M. H. Atwater, *Beyond the Light*[7]

The cosmic cinema is a glorious manifestation of the imaginary thought processes of God's Mind, but the projected light images of God's imagining, which seem to move and have life of being in themselves, are but electrically-sensed thought forms of thought imaginings that but constitute a mirage of the reality which they but simulate.—Walter Russell (1871–1963), sculptor, musician, author, philosopher, and mystic[8]

The "cosmic motion picture" is true not only to two human senses, sight and hearing, but to all five. It is presented to us three-dimensionally and includes the illusion of smell, taste, and touch. And yet, just as the light

The Physics of Miraculous Healing

emanating from the projection booth produces mere images of reality, so also does God's light produce mere appearances.—Swami Kriyananda, *Essence of the Bhagavad Gita*[9]

According to experiential spiritual teachers and near-death experiencers the local physical universe is more illusion than permanent reality. The holographic projection of the local physical universe that we experience today would vanish if the nonlocal holographic projection process were to cease—just as the image on a movie theater screen would vanish if the projector in the projection booth were turned off.

God is creating the entire universe, fully and totally, in this present now. Everything God created ... God creates now all at once.— Meister Eckhart, Christian mystic[10]

The universe emerges out of an all-nourishing abyss not only twelve billion years ago but in every moment.—Brian Swimme, physicist[11]

My solemn proclamation is that a new universe is created every moment.—D. T. Suzuki, Zen teacher[12]

We are not stuff that abides, but patterns that perpetuate themselves; whirlpools of water in an ever-flowing river.—Norbert Wiener, physicist[13]

The Tao is the sustaining Life-force and the mother of all things; from it, all things rise and fall without cease.—Lao Tzu, Tao Te Ching

We have sought for firm ground and found none. The deeper we penetrate, the more restless becomes the universe; all is rushing about and vibrating in a wild dance.—Max Born, Nobel Prize winning physicist[14]

Beholding the ever-changing sound-and-motion-pictures of life, I am aware that this turbulent dancing show is only a vast illusion.—Paramhansa Yogananda, yoga master[15]

The Physics of Miraculous Healing

Many people find it difficult to accept that there could be a higher Intelligence at work either in the physical world or in the physical body because they see no physical laws directly affected by such an Intelligence. They reason that if a higher Intelligence *did* exist, the evidence for it would be that physical laws were broken, and, instead, they see only the seamless working of myriad interconnected physical laws.

To my knowledge, the dynamic holographic process of M-theory offers the first scientifically sound and lawful explanation of how higher Intelligence can directly affect, at cellular or atomic levels, the minute processes that make life possible—without breaking any *physical* laws. How? By affecting *the film-like hologram only;* while physical laws—from classical physics to chemistry—directly affect *the holographic projection only.*

The holographic dynamic between the physical body and the subtle energy body integrates classical physics with modern physics without violating the laws of either. Intelligently guided coordination of the subtle energy body—which is the essential answer to many unanswered questions about the human body—integrates modern physics with spiritual teachings and does so also without violating the laws of either.

CHAPTER 6—The Body is a Continuous Miracle

A Brief Recap
There are key functions that a purely molecular-machine body can't perform.

A purely physical molecular-machine body, according to the laws of classical physics and molecular biology, is unable to perform two essential life-functions: 1. Reach the speed of molecular interaction required to achieve the prodigious output known for many essential life-processes, particularly protein production. 2. Coordinate the quadrillions of molecular processes occurring every second in every one of forty to sixty trillion cells.

The physical body is not physical.

The physical body is a matrix of uncountable numbers of subatomic *patterns of energy*. When the matrix is observed, the patterns of energy behave as three-dimensional subatomic particles that combine into atoms and molecules; when the matrix is not observed, the patterns of energy behave as two-dimensional coherent energy-waves.

> There is no object…without a conscious subject looking at it.—Amit Goswami, quantum physicist[1]

The Physics of Miraculous Healing

The local physical body is not independent.

The local physical body is completely dependent on the nonlocal subtle energy body, the hologram from which the local physical body is holographically projected.

> The three-dimensional world of ordinary experience—
> —the universe filled with galaxies, stars, planets, houses, boulders, and people—is [contained in] a hologram, an image of reality coded on a…two-dimensional surface.—Dr. Leonard Susskind, Stanford professor and leading M-theorist[2]

Seamlessly whole.

Although the body has both local and nonlocal aspects, both aspects are *instantly interactive and seamlessly whole*; there is no spatial distance between what is local and what is nonlocal and thus no time lag between actions and effects.

> An organic whole is an *entangled* whole, where part and whole, [nonlocal] and local are so thoroughly implicated as to be indistinguishable….—Mae-Wan Ho, geneticist and quantum biologist[3]

Holographic interaction breaks the molecular speed limit.

The holographic interaction between the local physical body and the nonlocal subtle energy body enables routine life-processes such as protein production to exceed the physical speed limit of molecular interactions; it also enables the extraordinarily rapid physical change characteristic of miraculous healing.

Higher Intelligence coordinates all life-processes.

The missing coordination of the astronomically numerous cellular-level life-processes occurring every moment in the physical body is found in *higher Intelligence* working through the hologram-subtle energy body.

> A subtle spiritual mechanism is hidden just behind the bodily structure.—Sri Yukteswar, yoga master[4]

The Physics of Miraculous Healing

The Body is a Continuous Miracle

The everyday existence of the physical body is just as much a miracle as is extraordinarily rapid healing or recovery from terminal diseases. The everyday existence of the physical body depends just as much on the Intelligent coordination of the nonlocal hologram-subtle energy body as does the extraordinarily rapid change of the physical body experienced by Barbara Cummiskey, or healing from diseases considered incurable, such as experienced by Anita Moorjani and Mr. Wright. Although *rare and dramatic,* those healings were enabled by the *same laws* that in every moment create and sustain *everyone's* body.

What sets extraordinary healings apart from the routine functioning of most people's bodies is not the result of *different laws* than those that govern everyone's body; what sets extraordinary healing apart is the extraordinary use of *innate soul powers*—*emotion, belief,* and *connection to Spirit*—that *influence* the same laws that create and sustain everyone's body.

Anita Moorjani's *unusually strong* emotion of fear slowly but steadily killed her and her *unconditional embrace* of love brought her back to life. Mr. Wright's *complete and unquestioning* belief in Krebiozen cured him rapidly and, alas, killed him just as rapidly when he believed Krebiozen had failed him. Barbara Cummiskey's *dynamically real and heart-felt* connection to Spirit through years of deep prayer and communion with Spirit cured her in mere minutes.

We Can Learn to Deliberately Use Our Innate Soul Powers

While everyone's innate soul powers influence the laws that create and change the body, we tend to use our soul power influences haphazardly and unknowingly. Most of us entertain a mix of positive and negative emotions that cancel out their influence. Most of us hold a mix of conflicting beliefs that dilutes any remarkable outcome they could have. Few of us directly experience Spirit on a regular basis and thus do not benefit from Spirit's transformational power.

We can, however, become more aware of our innate soul powers and learn to use them deliberately and methodically to remain healthy, to heal from serious injury, or to overcome disease—even those diseases considered terminal.

In Part 2 we will explore in greater detail how and why our soul powers work in the context of the Intelligently guided, holographically created body; how we cause—and cure—our own ill health and disease; and why no disease is incurable.

In Part 3, building on the understanding of our soul powers gained in Part 2, we will explore many practices and techniques that both increase awareness of our soul powers and enable us to methodically use them. These practices include awakening or strengthening positive health-changing emotions, increasing subtle life force, developing powerful health-creating beliefs, and consciously and effectively connecting to the core source of all health, the Spirit within.

Part 2

Understanding Your Soul Powers

CHAPTER 7—Emotion

Emotions have a powerful influence on our health. Studies show that when negative emotion becomes habitual, we are highly likely to become ill or die before our time.

The decades-long Grant Study followed two hundred and sixty-eight Harvard graduates for thirty years. Each year of the study, health surveys and psychological tests were conducted with every study participant. When the participants' health surveys were later compared to their psychological tests a highly significant correlation emerged: "Of 59 men with the best mental health assessed from the age of 21 to 46 years, only two became chronically ill or died by the age of 53. Of the 48 men with the worst mental health from the age of 21 to 46, 18 became chronically ill or died."[1]

Psychologist Lawrence LeShan, author of *Cancer as a Turning Point*, conducted a study of 455 cancer patients; the study included in-depth therapy with 71 patients considered terminal. He found that a condition of *despair* was reported as predating the onset of terminal cancer by 68 of his 71 cancer patients but by only 3 of 88 of his clients with non-terminal cancer.[2]

Stress, the *negative emotional reaction* to the pressures of a busy life—fear of loss, anger at unwanted outcomes, painful feelings in trying relationships—is variously estimated to cause *seventy-five to ninety percent* of all illness, including the two most prevalent causes of death worldwide—heart disease and cancer.[3]

The Physics of Miraculous Healing

But Why?
The connection between ill health and long-term negative emotion is well documented, but modern medicine has found no clear reason for it. Doctors appreciate that the beginning of all disease is that the cells that make up the tissues or organs associated with a particular disease begin to break down, lose function, become deranged, or—the beginning of all types of cancer—reproduce out of control and produce health-destroying, even life-destroying tumors. Yet modern medicine hasn't found any molecular mechanisms that can explain how chronic negative emotion causes cellular breakdown.

What are Emotions?
To understand the dynamic between emotions and health we need first to understand the source and nature of emotions themselves. You might think that the source and nature of emotions—such a commonly experienced human phenomena with such a significant influence on our health—would be well understood by now. But, in fact, different camps within mainstream medicine and psychology are in wide disagreement about emotion.

The basic-emotion theory has held sway since the early part of the twentieth century. The basic-emotion theory posits that a small set of emotions, such as fear, disgust, love, and joy, can combine in differing proportions to express all the emotional states that we can experience, rather like the three primary colors of red, blue, and yellow can combine in differing proportions to create all the colors we can perceive.

The basic-emotions theory also posits that emotions are *produced in fixed locations* in the brain, particularly in the brain stem, the evolutionarily primitive part of the brain that humans share with animals such as lizards. The evolutionary aspect of the theory is based on the notion that certain emotions provide survival advantages—for example, that fear kept us alert to predators and love ensures that we take care of our own—survival advantages that became hardwired into our neural circuitry, rather like automatic reflexes, such as the pain reflex that makes us rapidly withdraw our hand from dangerous heat before it gets burned.

In the last few decades, however, the basic-emotions theory has lost credibility, largely because new neuroimaging techniques such as fMRI have been able to locate, with greater and greater accuracy, the specific neural activity that occurs when people experience emotions. The new techniques simply don't confirm the basic-emotions theory. Dr. Lisa Barrett, highly influential and distinguished professor of psychology at Northeastern University and Director of the Interdisciplinary Affective Science Laboratory, puts it this way: "accumulating empirical evidence…is inconsistent with the view that there are kinds of emotion with boundaries that are carved in nature."[4]

What Barrett and other researchers have discovered instead is that we experience specific emotions in response to specific *situations*—situations that are unique to each individual—situations that *cause the brain to form neural circuits* unique to that individual. Situations might include: praise or blame from a boss, achieving or failing to achieve a personally set goal, a child doing well or poorly in school, loss of a treasured possession.

The formation of neural circuits that stimulate emotions in response to specific situations led Dr. Barrett to what she calls the *constructed-emotion* theory. In a lifetime our brains form many thousands, potentially millions, of situation-supporting neural circuits which fMRI scans show to be located *everywhere in the brain*. Emotion-stimulating neural circuits *often have no neural connection* to any fixed locations, such as the brain stem, long thought to be the source of emotion.

The discovery that emotional circuits are everywhere in the brain and have no consistent connection to the theoretical brain stem locations led Dr. Barrett and other researchers to conclude that not only are our emotions stimulated by uniquely constructed neural circuits rather than by evolutionarily hardwired neural circuits, but that *all* our emotional experiences arise from a general source which they call *core affect*.[5] *Affect* is psychology-speak for emotion. According to Barrett, core affect is the *raw potential* for emotion. Most significantly, Dr. Barrett believes that the raw potential for emotion doesn't originate from *any* specific location in the brain.

Emotion is Nonlocal

The absence in the brain of fixed locations for basic emotions and especially the absence of any location at all for the source of core affect strongly suggest that the source of our emotions is not the physical brain or body. The discoveries on the frontiers of physics and the experiential spiritual teachings that we explored in previous chapters both suggest that the most likely origin of emotion is our *nonlocal subtle energy body* and that emotions only *interact* with the physical body, they aren't produced by it.

Although there is no *direct* evidence that emotions are nonlocal, there *is* indirect evidence. If emotions *were* produced by the brain the experience of those emotions should be limited to an individual's physical brain and body. Many experiments have shown, however, that we can experience the emotion of another person; findings that lead to the conclusion that emotions exist beyond an individual's physical brain and body.

Psychologists Marilyn Schlitz and William Braud developed an experimental strategy using galvanic skin response devices similar to those used in lie detectors. In their experiments one person was hooked up to the device, the *receiver*. An *influencer* was placed in another room, completely out of any possible contact with the receiver, and would, at random times, try to influence the receiver *to feel either agitated or calm*.

> Various controls were set in place for each of fifteen studies, with a total of 323 sessions and 271 subjects. Even though the receivers had no idea when the

influencers were focusing on them, their skin response showed a direct correlation with the influencers' intentions [to make the receiver feel either agitated or calm] fifty-seven percent of the time.[6]

More evidence that emotions can influence someone remotely has surfaced through an analysis of social networks. In 2008, political scientist James H. Fowler, University of California, San Diego, and medical doctor and social scientist Nicholas A. Christakis, Harvard Medical School, published "Dynamic Spread of Happiness in a Large Social Network," in the *British Medical Journal*.[7]

> Your happiness depends not just on your choices and actions, but also on the choices and actions of people you don't even know who are one, two and three degrees removed from you. ... Emotions have a collective existence—they are not just an individual phenomenon."[8]

A *Washington Post* journalist summed up Fowler's and Christakis' findings: "[E]motion can ripple through clusters of people who may not even know each other."[9]

This...may be a bomb with a delayed fuse that is getting ready to explode in the very heart of materialistic medicine.—Dr. Larry Dossey, M.D., author of *Space, Time, and Medicine*[10]

We experience the emotions of others because, from the point of view of modern physics and various experiential spiritual teachings, we simply aren't separate from others.

> The notion of a separate organism is clearly an abstraction, as is also its boundary. Underlying all this is unbroken wholeness even though our civilization has developed in such a way as to strongly emphasize the separation into parts.—Quantum physicists David Bohm and Basil J. Hiley, authors of *The Undivided Universe*[11]

Emotions are Movements of Nonlocal Subtle Energy

According to advanced teachers in various experiential spiritual traditions, particularly in the yoga tradition, emotions are *movements of subtle energy* in the nonlocal subtle energy body. The very word *e-motion* conveys the concept of movement. The word emotion is derived from the French word *emouvoir*, to stir up. We may describe a positive emotion as making us feel moved, stirred, uplifted, or transported; we may describe a negative emotion as making us feel shocked, shaken, rattled, jolted, or agitated.

The experience of energy moving in the subtle energy body *is* happiness or sadness, love or hatred, fulfillment or loss. In general terms, *energy rising or expanding* in the subtle energy body is experienced as calm *positive* emotion; energy *descending or contracting* in the subtle energy body is experienced as agitated or depressed *negative* emotion.

More specifically, energy rising rapidly in the core of the subtle energy body is experienced as excitement or exhilaration, a feeling of being "up" or "on top of the world." Energy contracting in the subtle energy body's navel center is experienced as fear or anger. Energy moving downward in the subtle energy body is experienced as sadness, as being "down" or "in the dumps," and, if long lasting, as depression. Energy steadily expanding in the subtle energy body's heart center is experienced as the emotion of personal satisfaction or love. Energy moving upward and expanding in the subtle energy body's brain center is experienced as inspiration.

Emotions Affect the Execution of All Cellular Processes

Understanding that emotion is the movement of energy in our nonlocal subtle energy body is the key to understanding why emotion has such a powerful effect on our health.

We have seen in previous chapters that nonlocal Intelligently guided subtle energy, enabled by the holographic process, continuously coordinates all local molecular interactions, all life-processes, in all cells: atoms and molecules combine into proteins and other biomolecules; those proteins and biomolecules then become mind-bendingly rapidly moving parts in the physical body's quadrillions of life-processes occurring every second.

If we could see the subtle energy body, we would see waves of emotion moving within it—calm positive emotional waves stabilizing it, agitated negative emotional waves distorting it. And if we could see Intelligence at work in the physical body at a cellular level, we could see calm positive emotional waves supporting the efficient execution of intracellular life-processes or we could see agitated negative emotional waves disrupting the execution of intracellular life-processes.

An occasional day of negative or mixed emotions will not do our health much harm if we soon return to experiencing positive harmonious emotions that support the healthy execution of life-processes. But chronic negative emotions—such as fear, anger, hatred, despair, helplessness, frustration, depression, grief—will, over time, do significant harm to our health. Sustained agitated waves of subtle energy disrupt the execution of cellular processes resulting in cellular breakdown: cells which fail to produce properly formed proteins will malfunction; cells which fail to produce enough biomolecules to support overall bodily functions, such as digestive enzymes, insulin, or neurotransmitters, will cause the body to malfunction; cells which uncontrollably divide and form cancerous tumors will threaten the body's very survival.

Emotion is a Soul Power

A positive emotional life is essential to good health and the capacity to self-heal. Fortunately for us, we possess the innate soul power to influence our emotional life. We can't, like flipping a switch, choose the emotion we want to experience, but we can steadily and deliberately cultivate positive emotion and gradually make our emotional life habitually positive.

In Part 3 we'll explore practices and techniques that *directly* awaken and strengthen positive emotions—and in so doing

The Physics of Miraculous Healing

cause new neural circuits to form that will automatically stimulate those positive emotions and thereby build significant support for our health and wellbeing.

CHAPTER 8—Belief

Positive emotions support and negative emotions disrupt Intelligently guided subtle energy as it coordinates and executes intracellular life-processes. Sustained negative emotions disrupt Intelligently guided subtle energy in its coordination and execution of intracellular life-processes which can result in cancer, heart disease, or other extreme health conditions. Sustained positive emotions support Intelligently guided subtle energy in its coordination and execution of intracellular life-processes which leads to good health.

The preceding paragraph is true—but not completely true. Intelligently guided subtle energy can coordinate all life-processes to produce a body with good health only if the hologram-subtle energy body is *a template for good health*. If, however, the hologram-subtle energy body is *a template for imperfect health*, Intelligently guided subtle energy will coordinate all life-processes to produce a matching physical body with imperfect health.

Why, you may be asking, would our subtle energy body ever be a template for imperfect health? Because, unknowingly, and throughout our life, we have directly influenced it with the soul power of our *beliefs*—beliefs held so deeply that they are beyond our conscious awareness and control, beliefs formed from childhood conditioning, from what we have learned, and from our life experiences.

Put bluntly, if we deeply believe that we are likely to get cancer, we will likely get cancer. If we have a family history of certain types of cancer, or know we've had long-term exposure to carcinogens, or have been told we have high genetic risk factors for cancer, or are particularly fearful of cancer and so frequently dwell on the possibility of getting cancer—any of these influences could lead to a deep belief that we will get cancer.

Ironically, it isn't family history, or genes, or carcinogens that actually cause us to come down with cancer. It is our *belief* that those factors will cause cancer that manifests as cancer. Conversely, if we deeply believe that we won't get cancer—despite the same negative indicators—we won't get cancer.

Our deeply held beliefs have this power because they *directly shape the hologram template* that is the subtle energy body. Deeply held beliefs that we are likely to get cancer will make the subtle energy body a hologram template for cancer. When this happens, instead of the Intelligently guided subtle energy coordinating and executing all life-processes to produce good health, our Intelligently guided subtle energy coordinates and executes all life-processes to make our body have cancer.

I wouldn't be surprised if you are finding it hard to accept the degree to which our beliefs have such power. We are conditioned to think that the body is a molecular machine and that, regardless of what we believe, it is impersonal molecular influences that cause us to get cancer or any other disease. There is a surprising amount of evidence, however, that indicates that our beliefs are far more powerful than molecules.

The Placebo Effect

Let's begin with the placebo effect, a phenomenon whose familiarity hides its astonishing power: People who have a belief

The Physics of Miraculous Healing

in the potential of a drug to heal them, heal just as readily when given a placebo as when given the actual drug.

Think about that for a moment.

Don't be confused by the usual statistics surrounding placebo testing results—such as, "53% of placebo users responded as well as those who received the actual drug." A 53% positive response rate doesn't mean that the placebo was only 53% effective, it means that for 53% of the recipients of the placebo it was *one hundred percent as effective* as the real drug or treatment. Nor is the positive effect of the placebo minor or temporary. It can cure people of anything that drugs, treatment, or surgery can—including cancer!

In 1968, researchers Luparello and Bleeker conducted a medical trial for asthma inhalers. Forty asthma sufferers were given inhalers which they were told contained an irritant. In fact, the inhalers contained nothing but water vapor. Nonetheless, after using the inhaler, almost half of the test group experienced restriction of their airways and about thirty percent suffered full asthmatic attacks. The researchers then gave each asthma sufferer a new inhaler, which they were told contained a medicine that could relieve their symptoms. These inhalers, too, contained nothing but water vapor. Nonetheless, every one of the approximately twenty asthma sufferers that reacted to the nonexistent irritant recovered after inhaling the water-vapor placebo that they believed contained the drug being trialed.[1]

Dr. Bruce Moseley and his team at the Baylor School of Medicine conducted a study of one hundred and eighty patients with *severe, debilitating knee pain*. The patients were divided into three groups: one to receive debridement—shaving damaged tissue inside the knee joint; a second to receive lavage—flushing irritants out of the knee joint; and the third was the placebo group—they were treated just as were the others (sedated, incised, and sutured), but none received debridement or lavage. All three groups were given the same postoperative care and given the same recommended exercises to help with recovery.

The Physics of Miraculous Healing

After twenty-four months *the percentage of positive outcomes was the same* for all three groups.[2]

Often over fifty percent of trial participants who received a placebo drug or treatment have positive results. The knee surgery study demonstrates that placebo treatment can be and often is just as effective *as the trial drug or procedure*.

Placebo recipients also often experience the expected *negative* side-effects of the drug being trialed. In 1976, a randomized, controlled study of a potential chemotherapy treatment for *gastric cancer* was conducted by the British stomach cancer group. The results of the study were published in the May 1983 *World Journal of Surgery*.[3] Four hundred and eleven patients participated in a double-blind study that involved the use of placebos. During the course of the several month's long study, thirty percent of the patients who were given the placebo/saline drip treatment not only saw improvement in their cancer but also *lost all their hair*.

Nor is it only in placebo testing that we can see the power of people's beliefs regarding drugs. An experiment was conducted in which ten men were put in a hospital ward for the night. All the men were told that they were being given a sleeping pill. Nine of the men *were* given a sleeping pill. Unknown to the tenth man, however, he was given a stimulant rather than a sleeping pill. Nonetheless, the man given the stimulant slept through the night with the other nine men. The reverse experiment was also conducted. All ten men were told that they were being given a stimulant. Nine of the men *were* given a stimulant. Unknown to the tenth man, however, he was given a sleeping pill rather than a stimulant. Nonetheless, the man given the sleeping pill stayed awake all night with the other nine men.[4]

Popular Belief Drives Individual Belief

There is a revealing and significant correlation between the *degree of popular belief* in the potential success of a trialed drug and the *degree of effectiveness of the placebo* in that trial. Irving Kirsh, in his book *The Emperor's New Drugs*, explores the data from clinical trials conducted over a twenty-year period by six major pharmaceutical companies that developed and sold antidepressants. The time period of the trials was also one of growing popular belief in the effectiveness of antidepressants. He found that the percentage of effectiveness of the placebo grew over time *in direct proportion* to the growth of popular belief in the effectiveness of antidepressants.

Rapid Physical Change Among Multiple-Personality Sufferers

Because our beliefs about our body, health, and health treatments usually change slowly, if at all, during a lifetime, we are generally not aware of how much these beliefs influence our health and fundamental physiology. What we experience are not sudden physiological changes but slow ones such as aging—a condition generally believed to develop both inevitably and slowly. Multiple-personality disorder sufferers, however, *do* experience sudden physiological changes; changes that emerge almost instantly when one personality transitions to another.

Dr. Philip M. Coons compiled the results of over fifty studies regarding physiological changes among MPD sufferers. He noted that these changes were measured by modern medical devices and techniques, including electroencephology, visual evoked responses, galvanic skin responses, electromyography, regional cerebral-blood-flow monitoring, voice spectral analysis, brain electrical activity mapping, and electrocardiography.[5] Measurements taken using these instruments as well as systematic observational methods leave no doubt that physiological changes emerge or vanish when one MPD personality transitions to another.

One MPD sufferer manifested needle tracks on his arms only when the personality emerged that believed he was a drug addict—even though no drugs had been injected. Rashes, moles, scars, and other skin conditions emerge and vanish as personalities come and go. A personality reacted to poison ivy;

fluid-filled blisters appeared on his skin. On switching to another personality, within minutes the blisters vanished.

One personality can suffer from allergies—bee sting toxin as an example—while the individual's other personalities do not. One personality can be diabetic, a condition that typically takes years to develop and insulin to manage, while the others are not. Each MPD personality can have different visual characteristics. MPD sufferers have been measured carefully by ophthalmologists for refraction (by measuring refraction errors or astigmatisms), visual acuity (by measuring focal ability, e.g., 20/20 vison), ocular tension (by measuring the intraocular pressure), keratometry (by measuring the curve of the cornea), and color vision (by measuring how accurately colors are detected).

In one study, a single MPD sufferer moved through ten personalities in less than an hour. An ophthalmologist was on hand to do a complete set of measurements for each personality. Once the results were examined it was found that *the eyes of each of the ten personalities had visual characteristics significantly different from those of the other nine*. These are not the normal physiological changes that anyone's eyes might go through over time from, for example, eyestrain or aging. It is as though the eyes of each personality belong to an entirely different body. In other studies, some personalities are colorblind for blue and green while the others are not. One personality has an astigmatism while the others do not. Even the color of the iris of one personality is different from the colors of the irises of the other personalities.[6]

Voice spectral-analysis reveals one's unique voice fingerprint known as a *voiceprint*. Even exceptional mimics, who can sound convincingly like many well-known people, cannot fool voice spectral-analysis; their underlying voiceprint remains unchanged regardless of the imitation they are performing, just as an actor playing many parts always has the same fingerprints. MPD personalities can, however, have a unique voiceprint for each personality. According to the laws of the molecular-machine

The Physics of Miraculous Healing

body, our genes determine the physical structures that give rise to our unique voiceprint thus for each MPD personality to have its own unique voiceprint, each MPD personality would have to be manifesting a unique gene expression—perhaps even unique genes. Although handedness is believed to be genetically determined, MPD personalities have been observed to write with different hands i.e., the left or the right.

To me the most astonishing example of extraordinarily rapid physiological changes among MPD sufferers is the 1992 case of a blind woman with ten MPD personalities in treatment with psychotherapist Dr. Bruno Waldvogel. Her blindness was confirmed through visually evoked potential (VEP) tests. When given an evoked potential, such as a bright flash of light in her eyes, no brain activity was detected in her visual cortex—something that simply can't be faked. She was blind. As her treatment with Dr. Waldvogel progressed, however, one-by-one nine out of ten personalities regained at least partial sight. One personality, however, remained blind and, when given the VEP test, continued to show no visual activity in her visual cortex.[7] One minute the woman was able to see to varying degrees depending on which of the nine sighted personalities was active—and in the next minute, when the tenth and fully blind personality emerged, she was completely physiologically blind.

How can these sudden changes occur? They occur because all the personalities of a MPD sufferer have *absolute belief* in their individual psychological, emotional, and physical identities. In the moments of transition from one personality to another the new personality's beliefs reshape the hologram template-subtle energy body and the holographically projected physical body instantly reshapes to match those new beliefs.

> Science teaches that we must see in order to believe, but we must also believe in order to see. We must be receptive to possibilities that science has not yet grasped, or we will miss them.—Dr. Bernie Siegel, author of Love Medicine, and Miracles[8]

The Physics of Miraculous Healing

The power of belief is perhaps no more clearly demonstrated than in the previously shared case of Mr. Wright, the cancer sufferer who had developed a deep belief that Krebiozen would heal him. The moment he received a dose of Krebiozen, his Intelligently guided subtle energy began to remake his physical body, redirecting myriad life-processes, perhaps even instantly holographically projecting new atoms, molecules, and cells, eliminating all effects of cancer, his tumors melting away "like snowballs on a hot stove."

When Mr. Wright's conviction was subsequently shaken about the efficacy of Krebiozen, his Intelligently guided subtle energy obligingly remade his body to be once again full of cancer, tumors included. When his conviction about Krebiozen was again strengthened by his doctor, who gave Mr. Wright a placebo that he assured him was an even more effective version of Krebiozen, yet again his Intelligently guided subtle energy obligingly remade his body in good health. Finally, when Mr. Wright some months later read the report that Krebiozen was useless, he lost all belief in its power; his Intelligently guided subtle energy obligingly remade his body to be full of cancer, and this time he died.

Today's Popular Beliefs Both Empower and Limit Healing Outcomes

Strong popular belief in modern medicine and its current drugs and treatments is a powerful creator of specific positive beliefs and subsequent positive healing outcomes—as we see in drug trials that use a placebo. The strong popular belief in modern medicine is, however, an equally powerful creator of negative, harmful beliefs and subsequent negative outcomes—beliefs that make us ill, keep us ill, or even kill us.

Mainstream medicine unintentionally limits potential healing by fostering and affirming certain deep negative beliefs: Modern medicine considers many diseases to be incurable—such as diabetes, asthma, arthritis, or certain types of heart disease—and considers many diseases to be terminal—such as lupus, multiple sclerosis, Parkinson's, Crohn's, lung cancer, and Alzheimer's.

In his book, *Love, Medicine and Miracles*, Dr. Bernie Siegel notes that many cancer patients told that statistically they have only a certain life expectancy died in conformance with the statistics. You might think that such conformance with the statistically average time of death by cancer is simply because inevitable and predictable rates of cancer-cell growth cause death in a predictable time frame. But Dr. Siegel also observed that patients *who believed they could regain their health despite the statistics* often lived on long beyond the average for their type of cancer—and some recovered completely.

The many cancer patients who died on schedule believed they would; they believed they would because they embraced limiting beliefs about health and healing. The cancer patients who outlived predictions or recovered completely believed they could; they believed they could because they embraced less limited beliefs about health and healing, beliefs that included the possibility of recovering from types of cancer considered incurable by mainstream medicine.

Our Beliefs Continuously Affect Our Health

Chemotherapy placebo-recipients losing all their hair, a woman MPD-sufferer who alternates between being physiologically blind and sighted, Mr. Wright yo-yoing between cancer and no cancer stand out so dramatically that they might seem to be special cases, but they are the results of the same nonlocal laws that continuously determine the health of *everyone's* body.

Just as all emerging MPD personalities unquestioningly believe in their psychological, emotional, and physical identities—so do we. Just as all emerging MPD personalities' beliefs shape the hologram-subtle energy body and cause the Intelligently guided subtle energy to holographically project their physical bodies to match—so do ours.

The Physics of Miraculous Healing

We don't usually experience dramatic physiological change, however, because our most deeply held beliefs that shape our hologram-subtle energy body rarely change. Nonetheless, our beliefs powerfully influence our health from day to day as well as determine how quickly and how well we will recover—or not recover—from illness or accident. If we don't believe that recovering from certain diseases or conditions is possible, we won't recover. But if we *do* believe recovery from certain diseases or conditions *is* possible—the door opens for us to do the things that will lead to recovery; if it is deep enough, the belief itself will heal us.

Believing deeply in unlimited health and healing, however, is not a choice made in a moment. Just as we can't flip an internal switch to choose a different emotion, we can't flip a switch to change our beliefs about our health. To develop deep belief in the possibility of unlimited healing, if we haven't developed that belief already, requires time, open-minded study, and personal experience. We must also release the tenacious grip modern medicine's limited beliefs have on our own. In Part 3 we will explore ways to use our innate soul power to deliberately and methodically change our health beliefs.

CHAPTER 9—Connection to Spirit

We are So Much More Than We Know

Our emotions and beliefs have extraordinary power over our body because they draw on the extraordinary power of the soul. The late Ram Dass often observed that we aren't human beings having spiritual experiences, we are spiritual beings having human experiences. Or as author Anthon St. Maarten delightfully puts it, "You are a Deity in jeans and a t-shirt, and within you dwells the infinite wisdom of the ages and the sacred creative force of All that is, will be and ever was."[1]

Is it not written in your law, I said, Ye are gods?—John 10:34

Born of God, we are spirit, and cannot be anything else. All is mind—one mind. We are that mind asleep—yet awakening, and God is that mind eternally aware.—Jan Price, near-death experiencer[2]

God wants us to become as he is, and has invested us with godlike qualities. I understood that he wants us to draw on the powers of heaven, and that by believing we are capable of doing so, we can.—Betty Eadie, near-death experiencer[3]

When we begin to understand the total being that is man, we realize that he is no simple physical organism. Within him are many powers whose potential he

> employs in greater or lesser degree in accommodating himself to the conditions of this world. Their potential is vastly greater than the average person thinks.—Paramhansa Yogananda, yoga master[4]

Although our extraordinary soul powers are innate, the conviction that we are nothing more than a molecular-machine reduces their power. Connecting to Spirit, on the other hand, awakens the conviction that we are a nonmaterial soul which, in turn, strengthens our extraordinary soul powers. By connecting to Spirit, itself a soul power, our innate positive emotions grow in strength, providing increasingly stronger support for the Intelligently guided successful execution of all life-processes; and our beliefs about health and healing become less and less limited, unleashing the power to directly transform the hologram-subtle energy body.

Connecting to Spirit Awakens the Most Positive Emotions

Connecting to Spirit awakens our awareness of the soul and thereby awakens our awareness of the most positive emotions it is possible for us to experience. We are, in our soul essence, joy, love, and peace.

> We are pure love—every single one of us. I knew that realizing this meant never being afraid of who we are. As I experienced my biggest revelation, it felt like a bolt of lightning. I understood that merely by being the love I truly am, I would heal both myself and others.—Anita Moorjani[5]

> Then I simply remember I became more blissful, more rapturous, more ecstatic. I was just filling and filling with this light and love that was in the light.—Jayne Smith, near-death experiencer, transcribed from the video, *A Moment of Truth*[6]

Experiencing the purely positive emotion at the core of our soul is the goal and the reward of all experiential spiritual traditions—and the common denominator of all spiritual experience.

> A sense of all-knowing enveloped me. Every part of my being was satisfied with an unconditional love beyond description. All questions were answered. An inner peace without striving or achieving was created and understood.
> —Laurelynn Martin, near-death experiencer, *Searching for Home*[7]

> We need to be alone with God in silence to be renewed and transformed. In it we are filled with the energy of God himself that makes us do all things with joy.—Mother Teresa of Calcutta[8]

> *Ever-new Joy is God.* He is inexhaustible; as you continue your meditations during the years, He will beguile you with an infinite ingenuity. [Those] who have found the way to God never dream of exchanging Him for any other happiness....
> —Sri Yukteswar, yoga master[9]

The deeper, longer, and more often we make the connection to Spirit the more we are immersed in powerfully positive emotions. The more we are immersed in powerfully positive emotions the less hold negative emotions can have on us. Immersion in powerfully positive emotions creates neural circuits that automatically stimulate positive emotional experience. The more neural circuits created that automatically stimulate positive emotional experience the greater the support our emotions lend to the Intelligently guided life-processes that heal us and keep us healthy.

Connection to Spirit Confirms and Deepens Belief in Unlimited Health

Our *strongest* beliefs about our health are self-fulfilling. They directly influence the template that is our hologram-subtle energy body. This template directs Intelligently guided subtle energy to

The Physics of Miraculous Healing

holographically project atoms and molecules that conform to what we deeply believe to be true. If we deeply believe that our body is dying, a dying body is what will be holographically projected; if we deeply believe that our body is healthy, a healthy body is what will be holographically projected.

Our beliefs about health and healing run deep. Because we have been conditioned to believe it from a young age, it is, unfortunately, most likely that our deepest beliefs about our health and healing conform to the health-limiting molecular machine view held by modern medicine. Changing such beliefs is not easy. If you don't already believe in your own divinity, that unlimited healing is possible, reading this book, or others like it, will help you build those beliefs. But reading is not enough. Nothing affects our beliefs more than direct personal experience. And nothing will confirm or deepen belief in our own divinity and the possibility of unlimited healing more than our own direct personal experience of Spirit.

> [A]lmost every belief I had embraced only hours before [my near-death]—that I was a physical being, that love was outside of me, that God was some patriarchal monarch sitting on a marble throne somewhere in the sky, that death was something to fear, that I was doomed by my past, that religion and spirituality were the same, that spirituality and science were different—was no longer true to my experience. Virtually every picture of 'reality' I had used to define my existence—not to be confused with my life—had been cremated. The ashes of the woman I thought I was were scattered on the wind."—Lynnclaire Dennis, near-death experiencer[10]
>
> All of a sudden, I felt more uplifted than ever before—I knew timelessness, spacelessness, and lightness—I did not seem to be walking on the earth. Every bush, every tree seemed to wear a halo…a light emanation around everything and flecks of gold fell like

> slanted rain through the air. The most important part was not the phenomena…it was the realization of the unity of all creation.—Mildred Norman, the Peace Pilgrim[11]

Belief-changing, belief-confirming, belief-deepening experience of Spirit is rarely as rapid or dramatic as those quoted above. But the same profound changes to our beliefs can build over time as the result of repeated experiences of Spirit in deep prayer or meditation. Whether slowly or rapidly, connection to Spirit will strengthen our positive beliefs until belief in the potential for unlimited health becomes the deepest.

Connection to Spirit Can Draw Extraordinary Healing Power

Connecting to Spirit can add extra, extraordinary healing power to our own, potentially resulting in extraordinarily rapid, miraculous healing. At first, miraculous healing may seem capricious, lacking any lawful process, favoring some and not others. But Barbara Cummiskey's miraculous healing wasn't capricious. It didn't come out of nowhere. She had quietly forged a deeply loving, serviceful, selfless, and prayerful connection to Spirit that uplifted her emotions, built a deep belief in the presence of Spirit, that eventually and dramatically, drew a powerful wave of healing power that transformed her hologram-subtle energy body which in turn transformed her physical body.

Those who have been miraculously healed had often built an unquestioning belief in the possibility of Divine healing before the actual healing took place.

> Declared a total invalid at age 51, Jean-Pierre Bely made a pilgrimage to the shrine in 1987. Bely was paralyzed by multiple sclerosis and had been in a medical condition that completely withstood any advancements in treatment since 1972. Without despairing, however, *Bely's faith in Our Lady* [italics added] as he made the pilgrimage was confirmed by his

The Physics of Miraculous Healing

miraculous healing. Many who accompanied him to Lourdes believed he would die before completing the trip. He even received the Anointing of the Sick when he finally made it to the shrine. Afterwards, however, he could immediately walk and has since made an entire recovery.[12]

For Jacob, overcoming stage 4 cancer took more than modern medicine…he needed an act of God. His doctors told him that his chances of living beyond the next four years were 30% to 40%. That's when faith kicked in. Boger says he made a conscious decision to entrust God with the situation, *"I had confidence that my prayers were going to be answered, and that God was a healer and was going to take care of me.* [italics added]" He decided to stop chemotherapy treatments after hearing God's voice tell him to stop. Shortly after, he became cancer-free. He encourages others to make sure God is moving in their life before refusing medical treatment.[13]

[Devoted nun,] Sister Bernadette Moriau…at the age of 27, began experiencing pain in her low back and underwent 4 unsuccessful surgeries. In 1992, she was fit for a spinal neurostimulator. In 1994, she began morphine medication. In 1998, she was diagnosed with sphincter dysfunction. In 1999, she began wearing a cervical-lumbar corset that would become a permanent necessity. In 2005, her left foot was put into a splint after developing equinus contracture. [I]n February of 2008, she made [a] pilgrimage to the Grotto of Lourdes. On July 11, 2008 in her community chapel a warm sensation fell over her. She felt called to take off all assisting medical devices and noticed that her foot had returned to normal. She then stopped taking her medications and ceased using the spinal neurostimulator.[14]

The Physics of Miraculous Healing

Such rare instances are not the result of Divine caprice or of the Divine favor healing one person rather than another. People who were miraculously healed held a deep belief in the *potential* for miraculous healing.

Connecting to Spirit is Possible for All of Us—Because All of Us are Spirit

Sudden, unexpected experiences of Spirit, of oneness with God, of Divine transcendence, are rare. While any one of us has the potential to draw such extraordinary experience, it is more likely that our experience will build with time; with patient, consistent, inner determination. But have no doubt, transformative Divine experience *will* come to you—because you *are* Spirit. And have no doubt that the experience of Spirit will awaken and strengthen your extraordinary soul powers.

> When we raise ourselves through meditation to what unites us with the spirit, we quicken something within us that is eternal and unlimited by birth and death. Once we have experienced this eternal part in us, we can no longer doubt its existence.—Rudolf Steiner, mystic and founder of Anthroposophy[15]

> This…power lies buried within you, and if you use it, there is nothing that you cannot accomplish. It is [this] power that has created everything—even your body.—Paramhansa Yogananda, yoga master[16]

> A single soul has the same power as God! You have exactly the same intensive power as God. You have the same potential as God within the human condition.—Mellon-Thomas Benedict, near-death experiencer[17]

Connecting to Spirit Does More Than Heal; It Overcomes All Fears

Many deep fears are born of the false belief that we are dependent for our health and wellbeing on the physical body and what we can experience through it. Such fears include the fear of losing possessions and financial security; the fear of being unsafe amidst rising crime, turbulent politics, and societal change; the fear of disease, accident, injury, and pain; and the fear of losing friends, family, and children to circumstance or to an annihilating death. Mystics and near-death experiencers lose all fear because their experience of Spirit brings the unquestioning certainty that they cannot die and that all is as it should be.

> It was enough to convince me totally of two things from that moment on: One, that our consciousness does not cease with physical death; that it becomes, in fact, keener and more aware than ever.—George G. Ritchie, M.D., near-death experiencer[18]
>
> I knew with total certainty that everything was evolving exactly the way it should and that the ultimate destiny for every living being is to return to the Source, The Light, Pure Love.
> —Juliet Nightingale, near-death experiencer[19]
>
> [T]he Self is Everything-ness, the All in which everything is known and obvious in its perfect expression of its own essence. One is total and complete, beyond all identities, gender, or even humanness itself. One need never again fear suffering and death.—David R. Hawkins, author of *Power vs. Force*[20]
>
> If I lived a billion years more, in my body or yours, there's not a single experience on Earth that could ever be as good as being dead. Nothing.—Dr. Dianne Morrissey, near-death experiencer[21]

Experiencing Spirit is not a choice made in a moment. Just as we can't flip an internal switch to choose a different emotion or to establish new deeply held beliefs, we can't flip a switch to experience Spirit. To experience Spirit requires gaining increasing control over the physical body and the mind, so that restless movement and thoughts don't draw our concentration away

The Physics of Miraculous Healing

from the inner experience of Spirit. In Part 3 we will explore ways to experience Spirit through the practice of meditation and to become ever more absorbed in the life-changing, health-changing experience.

Part 3

Practices and Techniques to Access and Use Your Soul Powers for Resilient Health and Self-Healing

CHAPTER 10—Setting Expectations

In the upcoming chapters we will explore practices and techniques to awaken and strengthen positive emotions, increase life force, develop belief in unlimited health, and make an empowering and transformative connection to Spirit. Before diving into those practices and techniques, however, I think it is it is important to set some expectations.

Thousands of inspiring cases of extraordinary, miraculous healing; the supportive laws and theories of physics; and the testimony of saints, sages, mystics, and near-death-experiencers should, I hope, leave you in no doubt that strong positive emotion, deep unquestioned belief in the certainty of a healing, and immersive connection to Spirit can heal us of anything, no matter how serious the condition. No disease is incurable and our self-healing soul powers have no limits.

But…to successfully awaken and use your soul powers for self-healing requires determination—and extraordinary healing requires extraordinary determination.

Miraculous healings are *rare,* not because some people have stronger soul powers than do others, but because only a very few people achieve the complete, absolute, open-hearted, determined embrace of their innate soul powers necessary for such rapid healing.

Anita Moorjani's rapid and unexpected recovery from advanced cancer was rare because her sudden and *complete* release

The Physics of Miraculous Healing

of fear and embrace of love are rare. Mr. Wright's rapid recoveries, rapid declines, and eventual death were rare because such *absolute* belief is rare. Barbara Cummiskey's extraordinarily rapid healing was rare because her *fully open-hearted and trusting* connection to Spirit is rare.

To successfully awaken and use your soul powers for self-healing requires not only determination but *long-term* determination. Although Barbara Cummiskey's open-hearted and trusting connection to Spirit healed her extraordinarily rapidly, she had spent many years, while seriously ill, faithfully building her connection to Spirit. Although Mr. Wright's absolute belief in the healing power of Kerbiozen in specific, and drugs in general, had dramatically rapid results, such a powerful belief would almost certainly have taken him time to develop.

Please don't think, however, that because it takes long-term determination to awaken and strengthen your innate soul powers that this approach to health and healing is unrealistic or not for you. The most important expectation I would like to set for you is that *any degree* to which your emotions become *more positive*, your beliefs in unlimited health become *deeper*, or your connection to Spirit becomes *greater* will improve your health and strengthen your innate ability to self-heal.

Keep in perspective also that your current emotions, beliefs, and degree of connection or lack of connection to Spirit are already powerfully influencing your health. Why not use your innate powers more positively and methodically?

And, if you are suffering from serious illness, keep in mind that every year many people heal from what are considered incurable, even terminal, diseases, by accessing and using their innate powers of emotion, belief, and connection to Spirit. If others can do it, so can you.

A Real and Lasting Cure

Making use of your innate powers to improve your health is not a quick fix but it is a real and lasting one. Steadily increasing the positive influence of your innate powers on your subtle energy body can give you lasting and resilient physical health and can *permanently heal* long-term, chronic disease.

Most common chronic diseases—such as asthma, type-2 diabetes, hypertension, arthritis, heart disease, and cancer—are caused by the breakdown of cellular functions.[1] Some examples: the breakdown of cells in the pancreas can result in the loss of ability to produce insulin which leads to diabetes; the breakdown of heart cells can result in oversensitivity to adrenalin which leads to hypertension; the breakdown of cells of many types can result in the loss of ability to regulate their cell-division which leads to the run-away tumorous cell-growth that is cancer.

Modern drugs *can't* restore the lost cellular function that results in disease. At best, drugs supply an artificial substitute for substances such as insulin that cells no longer produce, suppress unwanted symptoms such as high blood-pressure, or slow the spread of the disease by, for example, killing cancerous cells. But in most cases, managing such diseases requires life-long use of prescribed drugs.

Our innate healing powers, on the other hand, *can* restore lost cellular function because, unlike drugs, our innate soul powers directly change the subtle energy body. The holographic dynamic enables the subtle energy body to change the very atoms and molecules of which all cells are composed and to direct Intelligently guided subtle energy to successfully execute life-processes that restore cellular functions.

Overcoming Serious Illness

Overcoming serious illness requires more than long-term determination. We also need to heal our life. We need to become aware of and take responsibility for chronic negative emotions that we may have long ignored or suppressed; to discover deeply-held limiting health-beliefs; to open our heart and mind to a connection to Spirit that we may have resisted or believed not possible; and to make significant changes in the way we live our lives.

This requires a level of commitment that not everyone is willing to make but it is a level of commitment which can save your life. In his book, *Love, Medicine and Miracles*, Dr. Bernie Siegel identified three kinds of cancer patients:

> About 15 to 20 percent of all patients unconsciously, or even consciously, wish to die. On some level they welcome cancer or another serious illness as a way to escape their problems through death or disease. In the middle of the spectrum of patients is the majority, about 60 to 70 percent. These are the people who, given a choice, would rather be operated on than actively work to get well. At the other extreme are the 15 to 20 percent who are exceptional.[2]

Dr. Siegel observed that his "exceptional" patients took charge of their health. They became committed to experiencing positive emotions, determined to embrace less limited health beliefs, and open to experiencing Spirit. It was his exceptional patients that lived beyond the statistical time estimates of cancer survival or, in many cases, were completely healed from their cancer.

Kelly Turner, an oncology researcher and author of *Radical Remission: Surviving Cancer Against All Odds*, studied such "exceptional" patients—one thousand people who experienced radical remission from terminal cancer. After researching their cases, she identified nine common practices among those who fully recovered from terminal cancer. Seven of these work with emotion, belief, or connection to Spirit:

- Taking charge of your health
- Following your intuition
- Releasing suppressed emotions
- Increasing positive emotions
- Embracing social support
- Deepening your spiritual connection

The Physics of Miraculous Healing

- Having strong reasons for living[3]

Whether you have cancer, heart disease, or any other life-threatening condition, if you want to fully heal, you need to take charge of *all* aspects of your life. Not only can taking charge of your life truly heal the body, it has the wonderful bonus of greatly increasing your quality of life.

> Being a cancer survivor is like being shaken in a kaleidoscope. You grasp for your bearings, desperate to find your balance amidst the chaos. When the dust finally settles, there is a new constellation of colors that are magical and beautiful. –Renee Exelbert[4]

> I learned how to look at each silver lining without feeling like I was falling for a Hallmark card. 'Everything happens for a reason' was still hard to hear, but it became the only way I could survive when the bad news kept coming. Ultimately, I realized what a miracle it really is to be alive and to lean into mindfulness, being present, as the best remedy for truly enjoying life.—Stephanie Chuang[5]

> Facing cancer forces you to look inward, ask yourself hard questions about life, death, purpose, and gratitude, and it enables a new depth and understanding of how to live life from your heart, following your soul's purpose.—Sally Morgan[6]

Practices and Techniques for Ill Health *and* Better Health

The techniques and practices offered in the upcoming chapters can be instrumental in overcoming serious illness. The more committed you are to these or similar practices and techniques the more they will enable you to self-heal. You don't, however, need to be dealing with a serious illness to benefit. Using these practices and techniques regularly to experience positive, harmonious emotions, develop a doubt-free expectation of good health, or to find the profound peace of

The Physics of Miraculous Healing

mind that comes with connecting to Spirit can make you resiliently healthy and, if you do become ill or suffer an accident, able to heal more readily and rapidly than you otherwise would. Don't wait for an illness. Start now; it's much easier when you're healthy.

CHAPTER 11— A Note on Other Healing Modalities

There are many healing modalities that you can use to improve your health: diet, vitamins, and supplements; subtle essences from homeopathy to flower remedies; body work from relaxing massage to deep tissue work; life force stimulation from chiropractic to acupuncture; subtle energy healing treatments from Reiki to spiritual healing; and many more.

I encourage you to make use of any of these healing modalities. They can help improve your health. But don't let their use *distract* you from first embracing and making positive use of your soul powers—or distract you from making the inner changes needed to overcome unintentional negative use of your soul powers. Don't give these other healing practices the lion's share of your attention because they can't give you the lion's share of your cure.

Mainstream medical treatments can also be helpful but are not necessarily required. If you do take advantage of mainstream medical treatments, do so because, after weighing all your options, *you* decided they could be helpful to your condition. Be informed and in charge. If you do embrace mainstream medical treatments, especially if you are experiencing serious illness, it is important not to also embrace the limited healing beliefs that often go with the treatments.

CHAPTER 12—Awaken and Strengthen Positive Emotions

Awakening and strengthening positive emotions is essential to maintaining good health and to recovering from ill health. Positive emotions support Intelligently guided subtle energy in its execution of the many vital life-processes which maintain or restore the optimum cellular function of good health.

> The simple truth is, happy people generally don't get sick. One's attitude toward oneself is the single most important factor in healing or staying well. Those who are at peace with themselves and their immediate surroundings have far fewer serious illnesses than those who are not.—Dr. Bernie Siegel, author of *Love, Medicine and Miracles*[1]

Emotion is Moving Subtle Energy

As explored previously, when we experience an emotion, we are experiencing the movement of energy in our subtle energy body. We experience calm, rising, expanding movements of energy in our subtle energy body as positive emotions such as peace, love, joy, inspiration, or gratitude. We experience agitated, descending, contracting movements of energy in our subtle energy body as negative emotions such as fear, anger, hate, jealousy, depression, or despair.

Understanding that emotion is a movement of energy in our subtle energy body is key to awakening and strengthening positive emotion. We can learn to *directly* stimulate the movement of calm, rising, expanding energy in our subtle energy body; movement of energy that is usually only *indirectly* stimulated by specific life situations such as being loved, accomplishing an important goal, or gaining some new possession.

Most Emotional Experience is a Reaction to Situations
The great majority of our emotions are automatically triggered *reactions* to situations. Dr. Barrett's theory of *constructed emotion*, shared in a previous chapter, explains that repeated and consistent emotional responses to recurring situations has caused the brain to *construct* thousands to millions of neural circuits that, when triggered by a specific situation, *automatically* stimulate a specific emotion, automatically cause energy to move in a specific pattern in the subtle energy body. The result is that we automatically react with some degree of emotion, positive or negative, from slight to strong, to nearly every situation we experience.

Surrounding ourselves with the situations involving people, experiences, and environments that trigger our neural circuits associated with positive emotions will make the best of the positive emotional neural circuits that have already formed in our brain. But far more likely to make us steadily happy, and thus steadily healthy, is to not *rely* on situations that are largely beyond our control to stimulate positive emotions, but to learn to *directly stimulate* positive emotion.

Meditation
Learning to stimulate positive emotion directly begins with learning to meditate. Meditation makes us more aware of many things that don't tend to come to our attention when we are absorbed in our usual active life. One of the first things we typically discover when we begin to meditate is that we are

physically more tense than we were aware and that the body is moving restlessly because of that tension. We also typically discover that we are thinking about a kaleidoscopic jumble of things such as difficult issues with people, pressing deadlines, or plans for the future.

If we pay close attention as we meditate, we will see that our thoughts are accompanied by movements of subtle energy—thoughts of relationship concerns accompanied by a contracting tension, a feeling of heaviness around the heart; worries about deadlines accompanied by an uncomfortable knotted tension in the pit of our stomach; dwelling on plans for the future, perhaps a vacation, accompanied by an upward and expanding movement of energy in the core of the body.

Though awareness of physical tension, racing thoughts, and contracting movements of subtle energy may first be discouraging, if we persist, the magic of meditation will take over. Simply sitting still will bring a natural release of physical tension, and simultaneously a release of the uncomfortable feeling of contracting movements of subtle energy. As the contracting movements of subtle energy are released, our breath, which is interconnected with those movements of energy, will naturally become deeper and more relaxed. Deeper exhalations will be accompanied by further physical relaxation which will lead to further easing of contracting subtle energy. Deeper inhalations will be accompanied by a wonderful feeling of calm energy and an expansive, upward movement of subtle energy—the essence of positive emotion.

The more we meditate the more we will experience the natural rise and expansion of our subtle energy. There is no need to *force* our subtle energy to rise and expand; we just need to relax and let it. That rise and expansion of subtle energy is experienced in many ways; as peace, contentment, love, and, especially, joy. In time we can experience joyful energy opening the heart, flooding the mind, and saturating our being.

> The highest experience man can have is to feel that Bliss in which every other aspect of Divinity—love, wisdom, immortality—is fully contained.—Paramhansa Yogananda, yoga master[2]
>
> In our ordinary life this truth is hidden from us or only dimly glimpsed at times or imperfectly held and conceived. But if we learn to live within, we infallibly awaken to this presence within us which is our more real self, a presence profound, calm, joyous…of which the world is not the master.—Sri Aurobindo[3]

Don't expect such a profound experience of joy to come quickly, but do expect it to come. Our capacity for such experience is an innate soul power. Put simply, we *are* joy.

When we experience joyful, upward-moving energy in meditation, it will tend to stay with us throughout our day and can to some degree counter any downward and contractive movements of subtle energy that are automatically triggered by preexisting, negative-emotion-stimulating neural circuits.

Meditation-born joyful emotion also causes new neural circuits to form that will automatically stimulate positive emotional experience. Over time, as more neural circuits are formed in our brain that stimulate positive emotion, the less often our negative emotional circuits will be triggered.

Meditation Techniques

I strongly recommend learning and practicing a meditation technique as it is difficult to withdraw awareness from our physical body and slow our thoughts without one. If you don't already have a meditation technique that you practice regularly, I unhesitatingly recommend the Hong-Sau technique. You'll find full instructions, including ways to sit, how to practice, how long to practice, and what you might experience, in Chapter 16—How to Meditate.

Be patient with your practice of Hong-Sau or any other meditation technique. Though you shouldn't expect amazing results in a day it is well worth sticking to your practice. When you begin to experience the first wonderful hints of your own joyful soul nature, and when you begin to experience improved concentration, lasting physical relaxation, a lift in your health, and an all-pervading sense of wellbeing in your daily life—nothing will keep you away from meditation.

Two Keys to Successful Meditation

There are two keys to making our meditation practice deeply successful; two keys to getting beyond physical distraction and restless thoughts so that we can experience our deeply positive soul joy.

Key 1: Stillness

Physical stillness, because it lessens our awareness of the physical body and increases our awareness of the subtle energy body, is the first key.

Awareness of the physical body comes through billions of nerves—within our body and at the surface of the skin—that send information to the brain. A region of the brain, known as the Orientation Association Area (OAA), continuously receives sensory information from those nerves, and assembles it into a three-dimensional, perceptual experience of the body.

As we become physically still, the amount of information sent to the OAA diminishes; our perception of the body becomes increasingly hazy until, if we can manage to sit perfectly still, the OAA receives no information at all, and our perception of the physical body simply disappears. Though sitting still is not easy and perfect stillness may seem far away, the closer we come to stillness, the less we are distracted by the physical body. Even a *moment* of stillness will feel wonderful, a feeling that will grow as our stillness deepens and lasts longer—until we feel the ever-new joy that is Spirit.

> Stillness is the altar of Spirit.—Paramhansa Yogananda, yoga master[4]

The Physics of Miraculous Healing

> Sit quietly, and listen for a voice that will say, 'Be more silent.' Die and be quiet.—Rumi, Sufi mystic[5]
>
> Be still and know that I am God.—Psalms 46:10

Almost everyone learning to meditate has difficulty sitting still. In Chapter 16—How to Meditate, you'll find guidance on the best positions to help you sit still comfortably, as well as breathing exercises to lead you into meditation. A tip for sitting still: Once you've begun to meditate, resist the impulse to make little adjustments to your position. After even five minutes of resisting physical movement, you will find the body letting go, relaxing, becoming more still. If time allows, yoga postures or other gentle stretches can help you release physical tension and mental restlessness before meditation. In the long term, regular practice of sitting still will also develop neural circuits that make sitting still more automatic.

Key 2: Inward Absorption

Inward absorption, because it calms the mind and slows our restless thoughts, is the second key.

Anyone who has tried to meditate soon appreciates the comparison of the mind to a restless monkey; train of thought after train of thought—regarding projects, recent news, interactions with others, upcoming events, future plans, concern over deadlines, recently experienced books, movies, etcetera, etcetera—not only carry us away from our meditation but often trigger neural circuits with associated negative emotions that make us feel uncomfortable, increase heart and breath rate, and even make us physically restless.

Physical and mental restlessness are interconnected; one stimulates the other. Remaining still removes the stimulus of physical restlessness but unless we also learn to simultaneously calm our thoughts, mental restlessness will once again stimulate physical restlessness. The best way to calm our thoughts is to become *inwardly absorbed.* Just as learning to become physically still will cause the body to become relaxed and free of restless movement, learning to become inwardly absorbed will cause the mind to become calmly focused and free of restless thoughts.

> Still the bubbling mind; herein lies freedom and bliss eternal.—Swami Sivananda, yoga master[6]

> To the mind that is still, the whole universe surrenders.—Lao Tzu, Tao Te Ching

To become inwardly absorbed we can make use of the mind's desire to be focused on *something*. Focus the mind on watching the breath. Focus attention at the point between the eyebrows where you may begin to see golden, opalescent blue or white light. Focus attention on silently repeating mind-expanding mantras or heart-opening chants. Pray.

Affirmation

Affirmation is another powerful tool for awakening or strengthening positive emotions. Methodical and concentrated repetition of a chosen affirmation creates or strengthens neural circuits in your brain that will automatically trigger positive emotion.

Find a wholly positive statement that encapsulates the positive emotion you want to awaken or strengthen; then say it and think it very deliberately until you experience it. Here are some examples:

> I remain ever safe within the impregnable walls of my inner peace.[7]

> I accept with calm impartiality whatever comes my way. Free in my heart, I am not conditioned by any outward circumstance. Whatever comes of itself, let it come.[8]

> In everything I do, my enthusiasm soars to embrace infinity![9]

Once you choose an affirmation, repeat it several times during the day. It is especially effective to repeat your affirmation at the end of meditation, when the mind is more calm, focused, and open. Within days to weeks of frequent concentrated practice, affirmation can form a new positive-emotion-supporting neural circuit.

Practice methodically. If you are alone, at first affirm loudly to get your own attention, then more softly, then whispering, and finally mentally only with deep concentration. Especially in the mental phase, *feel* the affirmation as much as you say it, believe it as much as you feel it, and, behind your believing know that your soul powers are giving your affirmation power to transform.

For a wide selection of affirmations as well as more detailed explanation and instruction, I recommend two books: *Scientific Healing Affirmations*, by Paramhansa Yogananda, and *Affirmations for Self-Healing*, by Swami Kriyananda. If you have other sources of affirmations that you already use and find helpful, by all means use them.

You can also carefully craft your own affirmation. If you do, be sure to be wholly positive. I also recommend including in your affirmation the recognition of your soul powers and the powerful support of Spirit: Rather than affirming simply, "I am unlimited joy," add a deeper dimension such as, "I am one with *Spirit's* infinite joy."

Above all, whether you use an affirmation written by another or craft your own, choose an affirmation you can *believe*—not necessarily something you think is *already* true of yourself—but something you believe can *become* true of yourself. Stick with *one* affirmation at a time—as long as it takes—until you feel its power within yourself, until it is no longer an affirmation but an experienced truth.

Some Thoughts on Negative Emotions

Awakening and strengthening positive emotion is the most *effective* way to limit the impact of negative emotion on your health and wellbeing. Awakening and strengthening positive emotion surely and steadily draws subtle energy away from expressing as negative emotion. The more often we experience positive emotion, the less often the neural circuits that stimulate negative emotion will be triggered; negative emotion is not suppressed or repressed, we simply don't experience it.

> [The] love that surrounded me and filled me was sweeter and finer than anything I had ever felt. I was changed by it, refined, rarified, made pure. I basked in its sweetness, and the traumas of the past were far behind me, forgotten and transformed by peace.— RaNelle Wallace, near-death experiencer[10]

Many schools of thought consider it necessary to work directly with negative emotions in order to acknowledge, process, and heal them. My belief is that we should be *aware* of our habitual negative emotions but working with them directly is slower and less effective than awakening and strengthening positive emotions. If, however, you do feel that you need to work directly with your negative emotions, let me suggest a few ways to make your process more successful:

Step Back from Your Emotions

Think of your negative emotions impersonally as movements of subtle energy—energy that can be rechanneled into more positive movements. Emotions aren't things. They aren't physically based. They aren't fixed. They aren't you. Emotions are simply moving subtle energy.

Avoid the Things that Trigger Your Negative Emotions

Emotions aren't produced by the brain; rather, the brain forms neural circuits that when triggered stimulate the movement of energy in your subtle energy body. Avoiding the triggers for negative emotions—behaviors, actions, environments, thoughts, and memories—will reduce how often you experience those emotions, and so will give you the emotional "space" to awaken and strengthen positive emotions.

Don't Wait to Awaken and Strengthen Positive Emotions

Don't wait to awaken and strengthen positive emotions until you have released all your habitual negative emotions: 1. it can take a long time to work through negative emotions and 2. a sustained focus on negative emotions can become depressing.

Cultivating positive emotions at the same time you are working with negative emotions is not only possible but will help you to release specific negative emotions more rapidly and more effectively.

Be Proactive not Reactive
Don't wait for favorable situations to *reactively* trigger positive emotions; instead use meditation and affirmation to *proactively* stimulate a rising flow in the subtle energy body. When calm energy rises and expands in our subtle energy body, we experience the most positive, health-and-happiness-creating emotions that it is possible for us to experience—love, joy, contentment, harmony, hope, enthusiasm, generosity, serenity, compassion, forgiveness, gratitude, appreciation, peace, security.

CHAPTER 13—Increase Your Life Force

Emotion and life force are two different ways that we experience our subtle energy. Subtle energy moving upward is experienced as positive emotion; downward, as negative. A strong flow is experienced as vitality; a weak flow, as lethargy. Emotion and life force are also interrelated. The more positive our emotions, the stronger the flow of life force; the stronger the flow of life force, the more positive our emotions.

Think of the physical body as a light bulb and life force as the electricity flowing through the filament. The stronger the flow of electricity through the filament, the brighter the light; the stronger the flow of life force through the body the stronger and more *resilient* our health. A candle flame is easily disrupted by a puff of wind but the flame of a cutting torch is unaffected by even a strong gale.

Health is not the absence of disease; health is the presence of abundant life force. If we have no bounce in our step, if we are frequently fatigued, bored, or uninterested in our life, we are not truly healthy and prone to develop disease. A strong flow of life force makes us feel great, prevents our body from developing disease, and, even if we experience disease or ill health, will enable us to heal rapidly.

Practices for increasing the flow of life force—willingness, relaxation, energization, and meditation—complement practices that awaken and strengthen positive emotion. Both work with our subtle energy.

Willingness

Willingness is the truest form of will power. Will power is often and incorrectly thought to require grim determination and tense effort. The relaxed and *willing embrace* of whatever is happening in our lives increases the flow of life force; grim tension reduces the flow. Those who enthusiastically embrace life as it comes enjoy a strong flow of life force; those who resist experience a weak flow.

Positive, enthusiastic willingness is common to all successful people—whether in business, humanitarian service, creative expression, artistic excellence, athletic prowess, or spiritual realization.

> My general attitude to life is to enjoy every minute of every day. I never do anything with a feeling of, "Oh God, I've got to do this today."—Richard Branson, billionaire founder of the Virgin Group[1]

> Nothing great was ever achieved without enthusiasm.—Ralph Waldo Emerson[2]

Even if other people see the work as hard, unpleasant, or boring, successful people have learned to be enthusiastically willing to do whatever needs to be done. They have learned to meet challenges with optimism, focus, and complete attention—and without mental or emotional resistance.

> Of all the virtues we can learn no trait is more useful, more essential for survival, and more likely to improve the quality of life than the ability to transform adversity into an enjoyable challenge.—Mihaly Csíkszentmihályi, author of *Flow: The Psychology of Optimal Experience*[3]

Walter Russell was an impressionist painter, sculptor, musician, author, motivational speaker, and exponent of experiential spirituality. His creative output was varied and prodigious. From the 1930s to the 1950s he was well known for

The Physics of Miraculous Healing

his sculpted busts of Thomas Edison, Mark Twain, General MacArthur, John Philip Sousa, Charles Goodyear, and George Gershwin. His biographer, Glenn Clark wrote:

> He…believes that every man should be master of anything he does, do it in a masterly manner and love it, no matter what it is, whether hard physical work, menial or boring work, or inspirational work.[4]

During my college years I worked as a summer laborer on a golf course. One day I was told to help move all the patio furniture from the clubhouse deck to a more secluded spot for a special barbecue dinner and party planned for that evening. When I got to the clubhouse, I saw that I was the only person there. I wasn't supposed to *help* move the patio furniture, I was supposed to move it all myself.

At that moment several of what I now know to be my own self-created mental and emotional habits automatically kicked in. As I surveyed the dozen large round metal tables with umbrellas, heavy umbrella stands, and forty-eight metal chairs, a train of negative justifications began: it was *unfair* to ask me to move them by myself because *it wasn't possible* for me to do it alone. Internal circuit breakers turned off one by one until I was left with only a trickle of life current. My life force drained away; my earlier positive mood evaporated; I was left feeling only mental and emotional fatigue.

Try as I might to rationalize my resistance, eventually I had to admit there really was no good excuse. One person *could* do it alone. Grudgingly I began to carry chairs to the pickup truck I had come in. They felt heavy and awkward; I felt too tired for the task; I knew it was going to take forever.

Happily, after carrying the first few chairs to the truck, I was rescued by more positive habits of optimism and willingness. New thoughts and emotions arose: it wasn't *that* hard; if I weren't doing this, I'd be doing some other physical labor, so why not get into it? I figured out a way to carry two chairs at a time, how to roll the tables most of the way to the pickup, and, by creating a makeshift ramp, all the way into the pickup.

The more I got into my task the better I felt. My tiredness evaporated as quickly as had my optimism only minutes before. I began to feel a strong flow of life force. My mood lifted. The work went much more quickly than I expected. I actually felt a bit disappointed when the task was coming to end.

Just then—I had moved and unloaded three truck loads; the last load was ready to go—I was informed that the barbecue was cancelled. Now I was to bring all the furniture back to the clubhouse. I surprised my informant—and even more, myself—by saying quite sincerely, "No problem." I was immersed in the wonderful feeling of strongly flowing life force. He was giving me permission to stay in that flow for another hour or more. Little did he know that I almost thanked him!

This experience taught me a valuable lesson: No matter what we need to do, if we accept the task willingly, we will effortlessly be filled with the life force needed. We don't have to generate, make, or create life force: we have only to get out of our own unwilling way and let it flow. If we say "yes" to our life, embrace what is ours to do, the life force we need to do so will come naturally.

> There is no limit to the degree of the will and therefore to the measure of energy, that one can summon in any undertaking, simply because a strong will is not limited by the energy potential of the body. It draws directly from the energy of the universe. The greater the will, the greater the flow of energy. Remember it. Repeat it to yourself several times a day. This single truth can revolutionize your life. –Swami Kriyananda[5]

Relaxation

Physical relaxation, positive emotion, and a strong flow of life force work together and are mutually reinforcing. The opposite

The Physics of Miraculous Healing

is also true: physical tension, negative emotion, and a weak flow of life force tend to go together and are also mutually reinforcing. Enhancing any one—relaxation, positive emotion, or the flow of life force—enhances the others. By deliberately releasing physical tension, we simultaneously increase the flow of life force and awaken positive emotions. A particularly effective way to release physical tension is yoga postures.

Yoga Postures

Our emotions are reflected in our posture. If, for example, we feel unsafe, our chest muscles contract, breathing is restricted, and the shoulders, neck, and head are pulled forward, as if to protect the heart from attack. If the feeling of being unsafe is chronic, our habitual posture will be hunched forward; our breathing, shallow.

The reflection of emotion in posture can be used to our advantage. All yoga postures are *physical* expressions of positive emotions. Each posture can be methodically used as the antidote to specific negative emotions. Any yoga pose that expands the chest, arches the upper back, and is accompanied by deep, full breathing is an antidote to feeling unsafe because it awakens positive emotions that make us feel *relaxed and open to life*.

Yoga Postures with Affirmations

The system of yoga postures that I practice—Swami Kriyananda's *Yoga Postures for Self-Awareness*—adds to each posture an affirmation that reinforces the effect of the posture itself. The sun pose provides a good example of posture and affirmation working together.

> Standing erect, extend one leg out before the other, knee of the extended leg bent slightly, both feet flat on the floor. Keep the weight centered between the feet. Bring the arms up from your sides to place the palms together above the head. Gently arch the back, bring the head and arms slightly back, breathe deeply and, as you

hold the pose, affirm aloud or mentally, "I am free; I am free." Then repeat, extending the opposite leg.

The affirmation, "I am free; I am free," supports and amplifies the expansive feeling that comes with the sun pose and can do as much to release physical tension as the pose itself.

Deep Relaxation

The deep relaxation exercise brings a meditative focus to the release of physical tension.

> To practice, lie on the floor, legs straight, arms along the sides. Turn up the palms of the hands. Head, neck, trunk, and legs should be in a straight line. Do not use a pillow in this position; the flow of blood should be equal to all parts of the body.
>
> Remaining motionless, visualize the body surrounded by space—space in all directions, space spreading out to infinity. Now focus on your feet; visualize the surrounding space gradually seeping through the pores of the skin, until the feet themselves become space. Pause briefly, then visualize space gradually filling the calves. Move your focus to the thighs. Continue in this manner through hips, abdomen and stomach, hands, forearms, upper arms, shoulders, chest, back of the neck, sides of the neck, throat, face, and brain until the entire body has become space.
>
> When the focus of your attention reaches the brain, release from the mind all regrets about the past, all worries about the future. Rest in the infinite ocean of the eternal Present. Be right here and right now.

Although the deep relaxation exercise is especially effective after yoga postures or after meditation, it can be practiced whenever you like. Feel free, also, to remain in the state of deep relaxation as long as you like. Avoid falling asleep. The deepest benefits come only with *wakeful* attention.

The Physics of Miraculous Healing

Energization

Physical relaxation, by allowing life force to flow more freely in the physical body, *indirectly increases* its flow. We can *directly increase* the flow of life force by drawing it into the physical body from the subtle energy body.

Paramhansa Yogananda, author of *Autobiography of a Yogi* and widely considered to be the father of yoga and meditation in the West, developed what he called the Energization Exercises. Each Energization Exercise allows us to draw life force into the physical body through tensing and relaxing specific muscles and muscle groups—often in combination with a deliberate pattern of breathing.

> The electric energy which motivates us is not within our bodies at all. It is a part of the universal supply which flows through us from the Universal Source....— Walter Russell (1871–1963), sculptor, musician, author, philosopher, and mystic[6]

To experience how the exercises work, close your eyes and concentrate in the area where spine and skull join—the location of the medulla oblongata, the doorway, Yogananda explains, through which life force from the subtle energy body enters the physical body.

> Slowly tense right hand and forearm, visualizing or feeling that you are drawing life force through the medulla and sending it to the hand and forearm. Slowly tense harder and harder for two or three seconds, until the hand and forearm are vibrating. Now slowly relax the muscles and feel the life force in the muscles you have just tensed.

There are twenty-six specific energization exercises which can be performed in ten to fifteen minutes. Regular practice of the Energization Exercises has many benefits: one, more life force available through your day; two, the ability to draw life force from the subtle energy body into the physical body at will; three, increasing awareness of yourself as made of energy rather than matter; and four, strengthened soul powers for self-healing.

The Physics of Miraculous Healing

(If you wish to learn the Energization Exercises I recommend *The Energization Exercises DVD*. You can find it through Crystal Clarity Publishers: https://www.crystalclarity.com.)

Meditation
It may seem counterintuitive to meditate in order to increase the flow of life force. You might think that the practice of meditation, with its resulting physical stillness would *reduce* the flow of life force. Although it is true that as we go deeper in meditation we become less aware of the physical body, we simultaneously become more aware of the subtle energy body, and thus our awareness of life force is increased. Even beginning meditators can have significant experiences of life force: subtle energy rising through the spine and into the brain—expanding in the heart center—expanding beyond the boundaries of the physical body.

Any direct experience of life force in meditation leads to increased awareness of life force in daily life—more positive emotion, greater mental clarity, willingness to accomplish long resisted tasks, solutions to significant problems, an absorbing creative flow, less effort and more flow in athletic pursuits, and dynamic health and vitality.

Life Force has No Limits
> Use constructively the power you already have, and more will come. Tune yourself with Cosmic Power. Then you will possess the creative power of Spirit. You will be in contact with Infinite Intelligence, which can guide you and solve all problems. Power from the dynamic Source of your being will flow through you so that you will be creative in the world of business, the world of thought, or the world of wisdom.
> —Paramhansa Yogananda, yoga master[7]

CHAPTER 14—Develop Belief in Unlimited Health

We can deliberately develop belief in unlimited health and healing. To do so we can make methodical use of the same influences that previously—and haphazardly—established the mix of beliefs we now hold—*conditioning*, *learning*, and *experience*.

Conditioning

Childhood conditioning is extremely effective because a child's mind has no filters. Spongelike, too young to question or fully understand what they are absorbing, children soak up the beliefs of those around them. Conditioning doesn't stop with childhood, however. As childhood influences wane, the influences of popular culture wax. We are exposed to a near constant barrage of media that includes popularized science and medicine. Although age brings more filters and a greater ability to question, the unrelenting influence of popular culture deluges us with more information than we can process, subliminally influencing our beliefs.

Instead of being haphazardly influenced by popular culture we can choose the influences we want. Though the influence of popular culture is difficult to avoid—we can learn to embrace the best and leave the rest. We can develop a habit of introspecting about *all* our influences. Paramhansa Yogananda urged people to "plunge into introspection about every experience—good books, problems, religion, philosophy, and inner happiness."[1] Introspection gives us insight into both the positive and negative beliefs we now hold and into how specific influences are strengthening or weakening those beliefs.

Armed with such insight we can choose influences that strengthen the beliefs we want. Especially important among those influences are people. Find and mix with as many people as you can who share the beliefs you want to develop and strengthen.

Learning and Study
Deliberate learning can produce stronger beliefs than does passive exposure to popular culture or the influence of the people around us. We can find inspiration to strengthen our belief in the possibility of unlimited health in the traditions of experiential spirituality, in the lives of saints and sages, in stories of near-death experience, in books like this one that draw together science and spirituality, and in the testimony of people who have experienced amazing healings.

It is particularly important, if you are unwell or dealing with a serious disease, to strengthen your belief in your innate soul powers for self-healing.

> If a "miracle," such as permanent remission of cancer, happens once, it is valid and must not be dismissed as a fluke. If one patient can do it, there's no reason others can't.—Bernie Siegel, author of *Love, Medicine and Miracles*[2]

> You have the power to heal your life, and you need to know that. We think so often that we are helpless, but we're not. We always have the power of our minds... Claim and consciously use your power.—Louise Hay, author of *You Can Heal Your Life*[3]

> No doubt some medicines have healing power, since God gave herbs and minerals the power to affect the body of man, but medicines and doctors have only limited power and often reveal their helplessness in cases of

chronic disease. Convince your mind that all human methods of cure are limited in their healing power, and that only God's all-permeating, all-healing power is unlimited.—Paramhansa Yogananda, yoga master[4]

Affirmation takes learning and study yet further. An affirmation is a powerful, concentrated, and deliberate way to awaken and develop specific positive beliefs about health and self-healing. The key to success is to practice until you feel inspired and then *believe* your affirmation of unlimited health.

My body cells obey my will: They dance with divine vitality! I am well! I am strong! I am a flowing river of boundless power and energy![5]

The healing power of Spirit is flowing through all the cells of my body. I am made of the one universal God-substance.[6]

Father thought Art in me; I am well.[7]

My outer life is a reflection of my inner thoughts. Filled with the joy of God, I express His joy and harmony in everything I do.[8]

Experience

The core *limited* belief that we must overcome in order to have *unlimited* belief in our power of self-healing is the belief that we are purely physical beings. From this core belief come all other limited beliefs about health—especially that the body is inescapably governed by the molecular-machine laws of genetics, biochemistry, and molecular biology.

"You have hypnotized yourselves into thinking you are human beings…in reality you are gods."[9]

The most effective way to overcome the belief that we are physical beings is to have *direct experience* of our soul—and the most effective way to have direct experience of our soul is meditation.

This new experience bestows new enlightenment which places the experiencer on a new plane of

> existence. He experiences a sense of universality, a Consciousness of Eternal Life. It is not a mere conviction. He actually feels it.—Swami Sivananda (1887–1963)[10]

Don't expect such a profound experience in meditation right away; but do expect experiences that expand your awareness beyond the physical body. As you learn to sit more and more still, your body will feel less and less physical—lighter, larger, less solid, its boundaries less sharp.

As awareness of the physical body decreases awareness of the subtle energy body will increase. As you breathe you may feel subtle energy flowing up and down in your core—a deeply satisfying expansion of energy in the heart—energy rising into the brain. And more…much more.

Even more than learning and study, direct experience will overcome limited beliefs about who and what we really are—and will leave us with the unshakeable belief that we are far more than a short-lived physical body. Repeated experiences in meditation of our non-physical soul nature lead not only to a strong belief in our health and capacity for healing but also brings true-beyond-any-shadow-of-a-doubt realization that the end of the physical body is not the end of our existence.

> This Self is not born, nor does it perish. Self-existent, it continues its existence forever. It is birthless, eternal, changeless, and ever the same.—Krishna speaking to Arjuna, Bhagavad Gita 2:20[11]
>
> By [meditation], one can reach the point of relaxing the heart, and thereby rising above its compulsion to outwardness, experiencing death consciously, and *eliminating one's sense of the mystery of death and the fear of dying* [Italics added]. One can learn, indeed, to leave his body voluntarily and blissfully, instead of being thrown out of it forcefully, often as a complete surprise, at death.—Paramhansa Yoagananda, yoga master[12]

The Physics of Miraculous Healing

Once we believe deeply that we live on beyond the body, that we are eternal, we release many primal fears—fears that negatively affect our health, that block our willingness to live our lives fully. Our understanding of the purpose of the physical body, of who and what we really are, changes fundamentally.

We are so much more than we know.

> At death, you forget all the limitations of the physical body and realize how free you are. For the first few seconds there is a sense of fear – fear of the unknown, of something unfamiliar to the consciousness. But after that comes a great realization: the soul feels a joyous sense of relief and freedom. You know that you exist apart from the mortal body.—Paramhansa Yogananda, yoga master[13]

CHAPTER 15—Connect with Spirit

Although Divine power is always working in us through emotion and belief, when we connect to Spirit our soul powers are strengthened, even supercharged. The more deeply we connect to Spirit the stronger our positive emotions grow, the freer the flow of life force, and the more unshakeable our belief in our capacity for good health and healing.

Spirit, God, Source, Infinite Mind, Divinity, Heavenly Father, Sacred Mother, Great Self or any one of many other names—is accessible to everyone. Our inner experience of Spirit can be enchantingly varied as Love, Joy, Peace, Energy, Light, Sound, Oneness, Eternity, Bliss—but the experiences are all unmistakably One.

> That light is the very essence, the heart and soul, the all-consuming consummation of ecstatic ecstasy. It is a million suns of compressed love dissolving everything unto itself, annihilating thought and cell, vaporizing humanness and history, into the one great brilliance of all that is and all that ever was and all that ever will be. You know it's God.
> No one has to tell you.
> You know.—P. M. H. Atwater, near-death experiencer[1]

> A kind of waking trance (this for lack of a better word) I have frequently had quite up from boyhood.

> [N]ot a confused state but the clearest of the clearest, the surest of the surest, utterly beyond words—where Death was an almost laughable impossibility—the loss of personality (if so it were) seeming no extinction but the only true life.—Alfred Lord Tennyson (1809–1892) Poet Laureate of Great Britain and Ireland[2]
>
> The body, the earth, the stars, the galaxies melted into a big unity—and I was a part of this unity. Unlimited and timeless my consciousness hovered in a pulsating eternity.—Frédéric Lionel (1907–1999), French philosopher[3]
>
> One becomes wholly Mind, the One Mind of God, in which exists all-knowledge, all-power, and all-presence.—Walter Russell (1871-1963), sculptor, musician, author, philosopher, and mystic[4]
>
> Oh, wonder of wonders, when I think of the union the soul has with God! He makes the enraptured soul to flee out of herself, for she is no more satisfied with anything that can be named. The spring of Divine Love flows out of the soul and draws her out of herself into the unnamed Being, into her first source, which is God alone.—Meister Eckhart (1260–1328), German theologian, philosopher, and mystic[5]

Even if brief, a deep experience of Spirit is subtly yet significantly transforming. Creativity flows. Intuition awakens. Life force is supercharged. Emotions are uplifted. Our best and highest beliefs are powerfully strengthened. The atoms and molecules in our body perform a healthier dance to the joyful inner music of Spirit.

> God is the Fountain of health, prosperity, wisdom, and eternal joy. Give your attention to the Almighty Power that is giving you life and strength and wisdom. Pray that unceasing truth flow into your mind, unceasing strength flow into your body, and unceasing joy flow into your soul. Right behind the darkness of closed eyes are the

wondrous forces of the universe, and all the great saints; and the endlessness of the Infinite. Meditate, and you will realize the omnipresent Absolute Truth and see Its mysterious workings in your life and in all the glories of creation.—Paramhansa Yogananda, yoga master[6]

Making a Personal Connection to Spirit

Many people think of Spirit as a distant, impersonal, and unknowable power incapable of or uninterested in having a personal relationship with us. If you hold such beliefs, I urge you to experiment, to open yourself, in a spirit of adventure, to a personal experience of Spirit. You have much to gain and nothing to lose by trying to make a personal connection with Spirit.

When, new to meditation, I discovered the teaching that Spirit is knowable, loving, and personal, I was inspired at a particularly quiet and emotionally open moment to ask within myself the simple question: "Are You there?" Immediately I felt a thrill of joyful energy radiating from my heart throughout my body. I was deeply moved.

We have only to knock and the door will open. But I will add a caveat to that deep truth. We have only to knock, *when our mind is still and our heart is receptive,* and the door will open. Stilling our mind can be achieved through meditation. Opening our heart is up to us.

> ...you can actually obtain God perception. In that way you can see, hear and play with God. Perhaps this may sound weird, but God is really there next to you.— George Harrison[7]

> [This radiant being] loved me in a way that I had never known that love could possibly be. He was a concentrated field of energy, radiant in splendor indescribable, except to say goodness and love. This was more loving than one can imagine...it was loving me with overwhelming power.—Howard Storm, near-death experiencer[8]

The Physics of Miraculous Healing

> God is Eternal Bliss. His being is love, wisdom, and joy. He is both impersonal and personal....—Paramhansa Yogananda, yoga master[9]
>
> This dance is the joy of existence. I am filled with you.—Rumi, Sufi mystic [10]

Prayers

Those drawn to a personal relationship to Spirit are also likely drawn to prayer. Let your prayers be a personal expression of your thoughts and emotion. There is no need for weighty formal prayers. Pray to Spirit as if talking to the wisest, most non-judgmental, even playful friend with whom you can share your inmost feelings.

> Don't be formal with God. Play with Him. Tease Him if you like. Scold Him if you feel to—though always with love. Remember, He is your very own. He is the Nearest of the near, the Dearest of the dear. He is closer to you than the very thoughts with which you pray to Him."—Paramhansa Yogananda, yoga master[11]

Make contact first

Prayer will be more effective if you first make soul contact with Spirit. Meditate. Become physically, mentally, and emotionally relaxed. Once you feel the Presence then share your prayerful thoughts and feelings.

Wait for an answering response

Deep prayer is a conversation. Though you may be blessed to *hear or see* a response it is more likely that you will *feel* it. Almost impossible to describe, the Divine response when experienced is *unmistakable*. You will feel happier, calmer, more joyful, loved, relaxed, safe, secure.

Pray for a deeper connection to Spirit

Most important is to pray for deeper connection to Spirit. Put that prayer request first, before any for health or prosperity.

Pray for others

The Physics of Miraculous Healing

Praying for other makes us a channel for Divine Blessings. The more sincere and earnest your prayers for others the more you will experience those Blessings flowing through you. Barbara Cummiskey prayed with such depth for others that those Blessings, even as they flowed through her, healed her.

Pray believing

If you pray for your own health, pray believing that your prayer will be answered because you are one with Spirit—everything that Spirit has, you have, too. You are deserving of all there is because you *are* all that is. Following are examples of prayers that contain this attitude of oneness with Spirit. If you use these prayers, make them your own, let the thoughts expressed come from your heart; believe every word you pray.

> O mighty Source of all that is right and good, help me to see my strength as an expression of Thy infinite power. Let me banish the darkness of disease: It is forever foreign to Thy light![12]

> O Father, Thine unlimited and all healing power is in me. Manifest Thy light through the darkness of my ignorance. Wherever this healing light is present, there is perfection. Therefore, perfection is in me.[13]

Devotion

To many, devotion—offering your earnest heart's love to Spirit—is a foreign and unsettling concept—something passive and mindless. Real devotion, however, is far from passive or mindless. Real devotion is the heart-felt and clear-minded *determination* to deeply experience Spirit.

Devotion can perhaps be best understood by comparing it to how we succeed at *anything*. Musicians, athletes, scientists, inventors, entrepreneurs, or artists—all those attempting to succeed—must love what they are doing, must be passionate about it, and be determined to succeed. Determination is the driving force of devotion; love for the Divine is the quality through which that determination is channeled.

The Physics of Miraculous Healing

Find a Source of Experiential Teachings

It is impossible to share everything that could be helpful to you to develop a connection to Spirit in a single chapter of a single book. Connecting to Spirit is the oldest spiritual art, inspiringly shared by many spiritual teachers through the millennia. If you already have a source of such teachings that inspire you, stay with them. Use them and go deeper. If not, find a source.

I found my source in Paramhansa Yogananda. He shared the spiritual art in a way that is easy to understand, accessible, and usable for me as a scientifically minded westerner. If you want to know more about Yogananda's teachings I suggest reading his *Autobiography of a Yogi*. If Yogananda isn't the source for you, reading his autobiography may well point you in a direction of your own. Whatever you do, find a source of teachings that work for *you* to connect to Spirit—and connect, dive in, immerse yourself. Nothing will benefit you more.

Part 4
How to Meditate and Establish Strong Habits

CHAPTER 16—How to Meditate

A wise man once said, "If people only *knew* how good they would feel if they meditated *everyone* would meditate." If you don't already have an established practice of meditation, you should get started. Meditation will not only improve your health and enable self-healing, it will change your entire life experience for the better. You may find yourself more open, considerate, lovingly compassionate, and more spontaneously helpful toward others. You may find yourself more centered and less emotionally reactive. You may find yourself flowing through your day with less resistance. You may find your concentration and productivity increased.

I urge you to meditate. Mediate regularly. Meditate as deeply and for as long as you can. If you embrace nothing else from this book, if you remember nothing else from this book, meditate.

How to Sit for Best Results

Find a sitting position that allows you to sit as comfortably as you can with the spine erect and the body relaxed. You can sit in a chair, on a kneeling bench or kneeling pillow, or cross-legged with or without a pillow. All these positions are equally effective. Deep meditators with many years of experience often use a chair for their meditations.

If you are sitting in a chair, sit with your feet flat on the floor. Your thighs should be parallel to the floor. In order to get your thighs parallel to the floor, you can put a pillow under your feet

The Physics of Miraculous Healing

if your legs are too short for the chair, or a pillow on your seat if your legs are too long for the chair. Do not lean against the back of the chair. Sit with an upright, unsupported spine, but make sure you are relaxed. If you are not used to sitting this way, or if you have back issues, you can place a pillow between your back and the back of the chair. If you use a pillow behind your back, the feeling you want to have is that the pillow is supporting your upright position, not that you are leaning your weight against it. Try different pillows or move the pillow around until you achieve this feeling.

Your choice of sitting position should allow you to relax your shoulders and keep your head erect with eyes facing directly forward. Rest your hands with the palms facing up at the juncture between your thighs and torso.

If you would prefer to sit on the floor, kneeling benches can help make your legs feel comfortable and help keep the spine straight. Finding the right size and height is important. Padding on the bench seat often helps. Adding small pillows under the knees or ankles might facilitate your comfort also. Those who are more comfortable sitting cross-legged on a pillow can try the crescent-shaped or round meditation pillows designed to help with this position, but any pillow you have that makes you comfortable will do just fine.

If you sit on the floor without a meditation pillow, make sure your spine is still straight, your shoulders relaxed, and your head erect with eyes facing directly forward. Your knees should remain close to the floor. If your knees do not remain close to the floor your spine will bend. You should also be able to place your hands comfortably, palms facing upward, at the juncture between your thighs and torso.

Where to Meditate

If possible, set aside an area where you will not be disturbed and that you use exclusively for meditation. A small room, or a corner of your bedroom—even a closet can suffice, as long as it is well ventilated. The place where you meditate should be a little on the cool side with a source of fresh air to keep you alert and awake.

Brief Preparation before Meditating

Once you are sitting comfortably, I recommend doing two brief breathing exercises that will help relax and harmonize your body and breath.

Tense and Relax

Inhale sharply through the nose, with one short and one long inhalation, while simultaneously tensing the whole body. Hold your breath and tension for a few seconds, then exhale forcibly through the mouth, with one short and one long exhalation, simultaneously releasing the tension in your muscles. Repeat three to six times.

Balance Your Breathing

After you complete the tense-and-relax breathing exercise, inhale slowly, counting to eight, hold the breath for eight counts, then exhale slowly for eight counts. Without pausing, inhale again, hold, and exhale, once more to the count of eight. Repeat this exercise three to six times. You can vary the count according to your lung capacity, but always keep the count equal during inhalation, holding, and exhalation. Finish your practice by inhaling deeply, then exhaling completely.

The Hong-Sau Technique

It is difficult to remain physically still and inwardly focused—two keys to having the best and most transformative experience in meditation—without using a meditation technique. I recommend the Hong-Sau Technique. Hong-Sau is an ancient Sanskrit mantra. It means "I am He" or "I am Spirit."

Close your eyes. Wait for your next breath to come in of its own accord. When it does, mentally say *hong* (rhymes with *song*), drawing out the sound in your mind to match the length of your inhalation. Don't hold the breath. Exhale naturally. As you

The Physics of Miraculous Healing

exhale, mentally say *sau* (rhymes with *saw*), drawing out the sound in your mind to match the length of your exhalation.

Make no attempt to control your breath. Simply observe the breath as it flows naturally in and out. In the beginning you may be aware of your breath primarily in your chest and abdomen as your lungs expand and contract. As the breath grows calmer, focus your attention on the cool sensation in your nostrils when you inhale and the warm sensation in your nostrils when you exhale. Gradually become aware of the cool and warm sensations higher and higher in the nasal passages, until your awareness of the cool and warm sensations of the breath is focused at the point between the eyebrows.

Now also bring your closed eyes to a focus at the point between the eyebrows. Do not cross or strain your eyes. Your eyes should be relaxed, as if looking slightly up at some distant point. Without muscular tension, let your focus at the point between the eyebrows deepen, while continuing simply to observe the cool and warm sensations of the breath at the point between the eyebrows. If you find that your mind has wandered, gently bring it back to an awareness of the breath, to your mental repetition of hong and sau, and to your eye's focus at the point between the eyebrows.

Once you reach the point where your awareness of your breath is centered at the point between the eyebrows try to become as focused at that point as you can without inadvertently tensing the facial muscles or holding the breath in or out. Try to feel as if your entire being is focused at this point. When you can do so, you will find a wonderful world opening to you. I will describe below some of the amazing things that can happen.

To complete your practice of the Hong-Sau Technique inhale once through the nose, then exhale three times through the mouth. Then forget the breath. Concentrate deeply at the point between the eyebrows. Keep your mind focused and your energy internalized. Absorb yourself in the peace generated by your practice.

The Physics of Miraculous Healing

(If you would like to learn more about the Hong-Sau Technique, including guided meditations, you can find more at: https://www.ananda.org. Search within the site for Hong-Sau Technique.)

How Often and How Long to Practice

Try to practice the Hong-Sau Technique at least once a day for 15 minutes. As you come to enjoy it more, you can increase your time to 30 minutes, then to an hour or more—always leave time at the end of your practice of Hong-Sau to enjoy the peaceful and harmonious results. Ideally it is good to meditate twice a day, first thing in the morning, early evening before eating, or before you sleep. Find a schedule that works for you. It is good to stretch your time meditating, but don't strain. Doing a longer meditation once a week, about one and a half times to twice as long, will help you to increase the length and depth of your regular meditation.

What You Might Experience While Doing the Hong-Sau Technique

Difficulty Staying Focused on the Breath

It is quite common to have difficulty keeping your attention focused on the breath and on mentally repeating Hong and Sau in rhythm with the breath. If you have this difficulty, don't think yourself not capable or not "cut out" for meditation. It is a skill to learn just like any other. When you recognize that you are no longer watching the breath, simply bring your attention back to it again. You may lose focus many times. Be patient with yourself. Your concentration will improve.

Difficulty Not Controlling the Breath

It is also quite common to have difficulty allowing the breath to come in and go out naturally. You may find yourself deliberately breathing in and out more deeply, or holding the breath in or out longer, than if the breath were flowing naturally. If this problem occurs every time you meditate, try doing more rounds of the preparatory breathing exercises before you begin your Hong-Sau practice—tense and relax six or twelve times instead of three, do the balancing breath exercise six or twelve times as well. If you still find yourself deliberately controlling the breath after you have begun your Hong-Sau practice, you can stop your practice long enough to repeat either or both of the preparatory breathing exercises before continuing the technique itself.

Other solutions: try mentally dissociating yourself from the body by imagining that you are sitting slightly behind yourself and watching your body breathe. You can also consciously relax the area around the solar plexus: Trust that the body will breathe just as it should on its own.

Difficulty in Sitting Still

Everyone who is learning to meditate has difficulty sitting still. After you've completed the preparatory breathing exercises at the very beginning of your meditation, resist the impulse to make little adjustments to your position. If you successfully resist the impulse for even five minutes you will find that the body becomes more still. If you have time, as a further aid to releasing restlessness, you may also want to do yoga postures or other gentle stretches before you begin the preparatory breathing exercises.

Your Breath May Become Deeper or More Shallow

As you watch your breath you may find that your breath keeps the same rhythm but becomes more shallow. Or you may find that the rhythm of your breath slows and that both inhalation and exhalation become much deeper. Either is good.

The Physics of Miraculous Healing

Natural Pauses between Breaths Become Longer
You may notice that the natural pauses between inhalation and exhalation or exhalation and inhalation become longer. This extended pause is natural and positive. Natural because in physical stillness your cells' lessened need to take in oxygen and expel carbon dioxide causes the breath to slow. Positive because you will soon find these natural pauses between breaths to be very calming, relaxing, and peaceful. Enjoy these moments particularly, but with no attempt to hold your breath. Forcibly holding the breath, in or out, will throw off the calm and natural rhythm of your breathing.

Breath Rate Becomes Profoundly Shallow or Slow
As you become more adept at the Hong-Sau Technique you may find that you are breathing so shallowly or so slowly that it is difficult to be aware of the breath. If you experience this it will feel wonderful. It is possible that your breathing can stop altogether, although that generally only happens after many years of practice. If you experience the cessation of the breath for tens of seconds to minutes, you won't need me to reassure you that this is OK, because it will feel *utterly* wonderful. Nor should you be concerned that the breath will not resume—the slightest physical movement will trigger the breath to begin again.

Heart Rate Becomes Profoundly Slow
While practicing the Hong-Sau Technique you should not be paying attention to your heart rate, but for reasons similar to why the breath rate slows, so does the heart rate—in physical stillness your heart does not need to pump as much oxygenated blood to the cells nor take away as much carbon waste product. If your heart rate profoundly slows, you won't really need me to reassure you that this is OK, because it will feel *beyond* wonderful. People who have mastered the Hong-Sau Technique can go for extended periods of time with no heart beat at all.

The Physics of Miraculous Healing

If the idea of your heart slowing down or even stopping is scary, I want to assure you that there is zero chance that, while practicing the Hong-Sau Technique, your heart could stop permanently or be damaged in any way. Your heart will have slowed or stopped because your cells' natural demand for oxygen is reduced or has stopped. As soon as you move or inhale, your cells will call for oxygen, and your heart rate will increase or resume just as naturally as it slowed or stopped. The heart stopping is even more rare than the breath stopping. It generally happens only to the most advanced practitioners.

Your Concentration Deepens

If you haven't already practiced the Hong-Sau Technique, or a similar meditation technique, it may be difficult to imagine how concentration can become deeper and deeper, but with practice you'll find that as your body becomes still, and your breath slows, your flow of thoughts will slow as well. As the usual flow of thoughts slows, emotional tensions will be released, the body will fade from your awareness, and your concentration will become more and more one-pointed.

You Will Likely See Light

Even early on in your practice of the Hong-Sau Technique, you may see various colors of light in the darkness behind your closed eyes. The light may be perceived at or around the point between the eyebrows. You may see white, blue, or golden light, or a combination of all three. The light may form into a circle at the point between the eyebrows: a deep azure blue field surrounded by golden light, with a tiny white star in the center. This phenomenon, usually referred to as the spiritual eye, is mentioned in many experiential spiritual traditions, perhaps most familiarly to Westerners in the New Testament: "if therefore thine eye be single, thy whole body shall be full of light." (Matthew 6:22)

The Physics of Miraculous Healing

You Will Likely Experience Emotional Release
The Hong-Sau Technique enables you to relax at deep levels: physical, mental, and emotional. Emotional relaxation is generally first experienced as a sense of peace and wellbeing. The heart center in your subtle energy body may be closed against situations and conditions in your life that you do not want to experience. Deep emotional relaxation can feel as if a fist in your heart has relaxed or as if warmth is spreading outward from your heart.

You Will Likely Become Inwardly Absorbed in Subtle Transcendent Experience
When you have a transcendent experience you will have no doubts about its reality. There may be a sense of wellbeing wholly unrelated to anything happening in your life. There may be a thrill of energy rising in the center of your body that makes you feel energized, positive, and enthusiastic. There may be a feeling of sacred Joy or of the "peace that passeth understanding." Once experienced you'll know, as millions before you have come to know, that there is another world within you and that you are experiencing your Self in Spirit.

Suggestions for Strengthening and Supporting a Habit of Meditation

Create as Many Positive Associations to Meditating as You Can
Set up a place to meditate that is attractive and inspiring. You should *enjoy* your mediation space for any of a variety of reasons: it's beautiful; it feels peaceful; it contains pictures or objects that are inspiring to you; it reminds you of other spaces you've seen that inspire you. Once you've taken the time to make your meditation space as attractive to you as you can, just *seeing* your mediation space will become a positive stimulus that will make you want to meditate.

Make your meditation position as comfortable as possible. Once you have found the meditation position most comfortable for you, just *thinking* about how relaxed you have been in your meditations, or at any time when *sitting* in a similar way, will make you want to meditate.

Meditate at the same time every day. Neural circuits fire that make you sleepy just before your regular sleep time. Neural circuits fire that activate your digestion causing a gurgling stomach just before your regular meal times. If you meditate at a regular time, neural circuits will fire that relax the body, thoughts, and emotions and stimulate positive memories that awaken your desire to meditate just before your regular meditation times.

Other suggestions for adding positive stimuli that will trigger a desire to meditate:

- Activate favorite scents—such as incense or natural oils—just before you begin to meditate. Activate the scent at other times during your day as well. Soon just *smelling* that scent will awaken your desire to meditate.
- Play music that moves or uplifts you—such as chanting, singing, or orchestral music—for a few minutes before you begin your meditation. Play the music at other times during your day as well. Again, just *hearing* that music will awaken your desire to meditate.
- Read a short passage of anything that moves or uplifts you before you meditate. Read such passages at other times during your day as well. You will find that even a *memory* of that short passage will awaken your desire to meditate.

In all these ways—and I'm sure you can think of others—you will be interconnecting many positive and desirable *thoughts, smells, memories, sounds, emotions, and times* with meditating. If *any* of these positive experiences occur, they will make you want to meditate and make meditation easier.

The Physics of Miraculous Healing

Set Your Intention

Make a pact with yourself. Emphasize to yourself the importance of meditation. Make sure that your heart is fully in it. Visualize yourself being successful. Imagine how you will feel when you have succeeded. Imagine experiencing the expansive, peaceful, joyful feeling of the self in Spirit. Setting your intention to meditate with special care can make all the difference when your will falters—when you aren't having the wonderful experience you'd hoped for, when your life's demands are making meditation difficult, or when conflicting habits are stronger than you expected. Keep your determination focused on your meditation practice until it becomes as automatic to want to meditate as it does to eat or sleep.

Be Patient

It takes time to establish and benefit from a meditation practice. You may not reap significant benefits from your efforts for weeks to months. Be patient. Even if your new meditation practice takes a long while to give you its benefits—it *will* do so.

CHAPTER 17—How to Establish Strong Habits

Don't Try to Establish Too Many New Habits All at Once

I have offered you many practices and techniques that will help you make significant change in your emotional life, your beliefs, and your connection to Spirit. But don't try to establish too many new habits at once. Don't make the classic New Year's-resolutions mistake. Surveys have shown that most people do not achieve *any* of their New Year's resolutions because, in their enthusiasm, they take on too much change at once.

In the beginning, they take on their new resolutions with enthusiasm. But, after a few weeks, the constant will power required to maintain so much change wears on them. Enthusiasm is replaced by tension. They begin to feel less, not more, happy. Tension and discouragement eventually undermine their resolution. Their old habits reassert themselves because they no longer *want* to exert the will power to resist them.

Don't try to establish more than one major new habit at a time. We establish minor habits with little effort and almost

The Physics of Miraculous Healing

without thinking—where we store information on our computer, the order in which we perform our morning routine, how long we steep our tea, the kind of toothpaste we use. A major habit, on the other hand, is one that will require significant time and determination to establish, and needs, therefore, our full focus.

Focus on One Habit Long Enough for Supporting Neural Circuits to Form

Neural circuits form in weeks to months to support anything we do regularly. Neural circuits don't make us do things as if we were robots, but they do make doing things easier and more automatic when we decide to do them. And they last. Supporting neural circuits are actual physical structures in the brain.

For example, a regular meditation practice will form meditation-supporting neural circuits that, when they are stimulated, will make your meditation easier by automatically triggering physical, mental, and emotional relaxation; slowing the breath and heart rate; focusing your attention at the point between the eyebrows; and more. The more you meditate, the easier and more successful it becomes because of the meditation-supporting neural circuits your practice has caused to form.

Expect to put out more effort in the beginning. When we begin to establish any new habit we may not yet have any neural circuits that will support our efforts. Initial success relies solely on our will and commitment. Think of riding a bicycle up to a plateau. Getting to the plateau is all uphill and will require determination, but once you make it to the plateau it will be far easier to maintain a steady pace. Similarly, getting started with any new habit is an uphill effort, but once supporting neural circuits become established it will be far easier to maintain your new habit.

The Physics of Miraculous Healing

Be Strategic About What Habits You Choose to Establish

Ask yourself, "What new habit will give me the most overall benefit?"

For those who don't already meditate, establishing a habit of meditation will give you the most overall benefit. Meditation awakens *all* your soul powers. Awakening your soul powers not only subtly improves every aspect of your health and life, but it also empowers your ability to successfully establish more new habits.

For those who do already have an established meditation practice, the answer to the question of what new habit will give you the most overall benefit is going to depend on your weaknesses. If negative emotions are a particular issue for you, you may want to establish a practice of positive affirmation. If physical tension or low energy are particular issues for you, you may want to establish a practice of yoga postures or energization exercises. If negative health beliefs are a particular issue for you, you may want to spend concentrated time on books, articles, and videos that provide support for belief in unlimited health. If connection to Spirit is lacking for you, you may want focus on awakening a personal relationship with Spirit in meditation. Introspect carefully to determine your best choice. Once you make your choice, stick with it until you get results and fully establish this new habit.

Be Aware of the Power of Existing Habits

In general, don't try to *stop* doing something negative, such as becoming angry, but rather *start* doing something positive, such as becoming more peaceful. We are more successful at self-change if we establish new habits that support new positive behaviors rather than try to suppress unwanted negative behaviors.

Be mindful, however, of the power of existing habits. Existing, automatically activating neural circuits remain in the brain even if we have made the decision to move away from the behavior they support. Once a neural circuit is stimulated that supports an unwanted negative behavior it becomes very difficult to resist the behavior. Try, instead, to *avoid the stimuli* that trigger unwanted negative physical, mental, or emotional behaviors while focusing on establishing new habits that support or enable new behaviors.

Feel Positive about Your New Habit
Before choosing to establish any new habit make sure that you feel *especially* good about it. Your new habit should be rewarding in and of itself, not just the antidote for old negative behavior. Whatever behavior you choose to establish as a habit, you should look forward to it, rather than feeling it is something you *should* do—but don't really *want* to do. The more positive and rewarding your new habits, the more successful you will be at establishing them.

Be Realistic
Be realistic about how much of a challenge you take on. If, for example, you choose to establish a habit of meditation, when you have none today, don't set out to meditate three times a day for an hour at a time.

Know your limits and exceed them only by a little. Better to succeed at establishing the habit of meditating for ten minutes before going to bed than to fail at meditating longer. Better a small victory that builds your confidence, than a large failure that erodes your determination.

Be Methodical
Once you've made your choice of the most beneficial, positive, and realistic new habit you want to establish, it is time to methodically plan as many ways as you can to make your effort successful.

The Physics of Miraculous Healing

Be Clear

Part of being methodical is to be as clear, specific, and as exact as you can about your new habit. If, for example, you want to establish a practice of meditation, what meditation technique are you going to use? If you haven't learned that technique, how are you going to learn it, and when? What time during your day are you going to meditate? Are there other habitual activities that you have been doing at that same time? If yes, what are you going to do with the old activities? Do them another time? Stop doing them? If you are going to meditate in the mornings, what time will you meditate and for how long? What does that mean for your rising time in the morning? Do you need to awaken a quarter, half, or a full hour earlier? Where are you going to meditate? What space can you use to meditate that will be quiet and allow you to leave your meditation things set up? How will you sit? Cross-legged? On a kneeling bench? On a chair?

Don't Leap Impulsively into Establishing a Major New Habit

After working out the details of your plan for establishing a new habit, give yourself enough time to consider and *emotionally accept* your plan—one person might need a day; another, a week; yet another, a month. When you get home in the evening and you are tired, how do you feel about your plan? When you are doing your usual morning routine that you are planning to change, how do you feel about changing it? Are there other people who will be affected by your choice? Do you think they will be impacted by your new behavior? What will you need to do to make it work for them? How do you feel about that?

After taking enough time to thoroughly consider your plan, modify it if you need to. Be creative, even unusual in your modifications. If, after much consideration, waking at midnight for a half an hour to read books that will awaken or strengthen unlimited healing beliefs, and then returning to sleep, feels like the only possible way you are really going to read consistently, then do so. Choose a plan that you *most believe will work*.

The Physics of Miraculous Healing

Finally, set a specific date that you are going to begin establishing your new habit. If you have a choice, don't choose to begin establishing your new habit during a period when you are going to travel a lot, have guests for extended periods, or have particularly challenging demands on your time. If avoiding these situations means waiting indefinitely before you start then rethink your plan and be as creative as possible in adapting your plan to work with travel, interruptions, or intensity of work.

Allow for Occasional Failure

If establishing a new habit is going to be a challenge to your willingness, chances are you will falter a few times over the course of weeks to months before new supporting neural circuits develop to make it easier. If you have been unrealistic about never faltering, and then you do falter, you may feel that you are failing, or even worse, that you are a failure; your confidence will be shaken and your will weakened. By accepting in advance that you may falter you will be better able emotionally to take it in stride. Don't let a single lapse ambush your efforts with a strong attack of self-doubt.

It can be helpful to think about what you will do when you do falter. Perhaps allow yourself a certain number of days off, days during which you give yourself permission to falter because you "just don't feel like it." Perhaps allow yourself an out if you have unexpected disruptions to your regular schedule.

Think these allowances through carefully. Even commit them to writing. Once you begin to establish your new habit, however, stick to your allowances—and no more. If you make too many allowances, the neural circuits will take much longer to form and may not be as strongly supportive of your new habit as they could be. Nor should these allowances be permanent. In time, a new habit should be regular even if you don't particularly "feel like it," even if there are distractions or challenging situations in your life.

The Physics of Miraculous Healing

By now you may be telling yourself that this degree of preparation for establishing a new habit is too elaborate and unnecessary. I have found, however, that for some habits I wanted to establish, often the most important ones, this level of preparation was required. Otherwise I ended up like Mark Twain who remarked, "Giving up smoking is the easiest thing in the world. I know because I've done it a thousand times."

If you want to make *lasting* positive changes in your life it can be crucial—depending on how challenging it will be to establish a new habit—to support your determination with a methodical approach. Positive habits that awaken or strengthen your soul powers are life-changing, health-improving, joy-awakening, long-lasting, and well worth taking especial care to establish.

The Physics of Miraculous Healing

NOTES

Introduction

1 Moorjani, *Dying to Be Me*, 76.
2 Klopfer, "Psychological Variables in Human Cancer," 331-40.
3 Cummiskey, "Barabara Cummiskey: Her Astonding Victory."
4 Lourdes Medical Bureau.
5 Barasch, "Psychology of the Miraculous."
6 Thomas, *The Youngest Science: Notes of a Medicine Watcher*, 205.
7 Hildebrand, "Das Universum - Hinweis auf Gott?" 10.
8 Macrae, *The Scientific Genius Who Pioneered the Modern Computer, Game Theory, Nuclear Deterrence and Much More*, 379.

Chapter 1

1 British Society for Cell Biology, "Ribosome."
2 Chow, "Why Your DNA May Not Be Your Destiny."
3 Ornish, "Changes in Prostate Gene Expression in Men Undergoing an Intensive Nutrition and Lifestyle Intervention," 8369–8374.
4 Rönn, "A Six Months Exercise Intervention Influences the Genome-Wide DNA Methylation Pattern in Human Adipose Tissue," e1003572.

Chapter 2

1 Folger, "Quantum Shmantum," 37-43
2 Kastrup, "Coming to Grips with the Implications of Quantum Mechanics."
3 Goswami, *The Self-Aware Universe*, 60.
4 Popp, "Hyperbolic Relaxation as a Sufficient Condition of a Fully Coherent Ergodic Field," 1573-1583
5 Engel, "Evidence for wavelike energy transfer through quantum coherence in photosynthetic systems," 782-786.

6 Panitchayangkoon, "Long-lived quantum coherence in photosynthetic complexes at physiological temperature," 12766–12770.

Chapter 3

1 Carrel, *Man, the Unknown*, 197.

2 Spurgin, *Insights into the Afterlife: 30 Questions on What to Expect*.

3 Berman, *The Journey Home: What Near-Death Experiences and Mysticism Teach Us about the Gift of Life*, 34.

4 Spurgin, *Insights into the Afterlife: 30 Questions on What to Expect*.

5 Livio, "Description of Heaven."

6 Yogananda, *The Second Coming of Christ*, Vol 1, Discourse 10.

7 Jung, *Memories, Dreams, Reflections*, 295.

8 Williams, "Christian Andreason's Near Death Experience."

9 Carrel, *Man, the Unknown*, 197.

Chapter 4

1 Susskind, *The Black Hole War – My Battle with Steven Hawking to Make the World Safe for Quantum Mechanics*, 410.

2 Swedenborg, *Heaven and Hell*, 57.

3 Yogananda, "The Astral World."

4 Eadie, *Embraced by the Light*, 47-48.

5 Dicarlo, "Conversations Toward a New World View: Exploring the Human Energy System."

6 Besant, *Karma*, Sec 13.

7 Dennis, *The Pattern*, 40.

8 Atwater, *Beyond the Light*, 142.

9 Durr, Television Interview.

10 Swedenborg, *Heaven and Hell*, 57.

11 Yogananda, "The Astral World."

Chapter 5

1 Nbcnews.com, "Survey: Most doctors believe in God, afterlife."

2 Siegel, *Love, Medicine and Miracles*, 69.

The Physics of Miraculous Healing

3 Einstein, *The World As I See It*, 28-29.
4 Hoyle, *Evolution from Space*, 141, 144, 130.
5 Connolly, "World renown scientist says he has found proof of God! We may be living in the 'Matrix'."
6 Planck, "*The Nature of Matter*," 1797.
7 Atwater, *Beyond the Light*, 185.
8 Russell, *Universal Law, Natural Science and Philosophy*, Prelude.
9 Kriyananda, *The Essence of the Bhagavad Gita*, Chapter 2, Stanza 30.
10 Eckhart, *Meditations with Meister Eckhart*, 24.
11 Swimme, *The Hidden Heart of the Cosmos*, 100.
12 Suzuki, *Zen and Japanese culture*, 364.
13 Wiener, *The Human Use of Human Beings*, 130.
14 Born, *The Restless Universe*, Postscript.
15 Yogananda, *Whispers from Eternity*, #75.

Chapter 6

1 Goswami, *The Self-Aware Universe*, 60.
2 Susskind, *The Black Hole war – My Battle with Steven Hawking to Make the World Safe for Quantum Mechanics*, 410.
3 Ho, "Bioenergetics and Biocommunication."
4 Yogananda, *Autobiography of a Yogi*, 76.

Chapter 7

1 Vaillant, "Natural history of male psychologic health: effects of mental health on physical health," 1249-54.
2 LeShan, *Cancer as a Turning Point*.
3 Segerstrom, "Psychological Stress and the Human Immune System: A Meta-Analytic Study of 30 Years of Inquiry," 601-630.
4 Barrett, "Are Emotions Natural Kinds?"
5 Barrett, "The conceptual act theory: A précis," 6, 292-297.
6 Braud, **"Consciousness Interactions with Remote Biological Systems: Anomalous Intentionality Effects,"** 1-43.
7 Fowler, "Dynamic spread of happiness in a large social network: longitudinal analysis over 20 years in the Framingham Heart Study."

8 Penman, "Could there be proof to the theory that we're ALL psychic?"

9 Stein, "Happiness can spread among people like a contagion, study indicates."

10 Dossey, "Brains and Beyond: The Unfolding Vision of Health and Healing," 314-324.

11 Bohm, *The Undivided Universe*, 389.

Chapter 8

1 Luparello, "Influences of Suggestion on Airway Reactivity in Asthmatic Subjects," 819– 829.

2 Moseley, "A controlled trial of arthroscopic surgery for osteoarthritis of the knee," 81-8.

3 Fielding, "An interim report of a prospective, randomized, controlled study of adjuvant chemotherapy in operable gastric cancer: British stomach cancer group," 390-399.

4 Hordern, "Psychopharmacology: Some historical considerations," 95-148.

5 Coons, "Psychophysiologic Aspects of Multiple Personality Disorder, A Review. Dissociation," 47-53.

6 Shepard, "Visual changes in multiple personality," 85.

7 Strasburger, "Sight and blindness in the same person: Gating in the visual system," 178-85.

8 Siegel, *Love, Medicine and Miracles*, 36.

Chapter 9

1 St. Maarten, *Divine Living: The Essential Guide to Your True Destiny*, 49.

2 Price, *The Other Side of Death*, 63.

3 Eadie, *Embraced by the light*, 61.

4 Yogananda, *Where There is Light*, 3.

5 Moorjani, *Dying to Be Me*, 76.

6 Smith, "Moment of Truth: A Window On Life After Death."

7 Martin, *Searching for Home: A Personal Journey of Transformation and Healing after a Near-Death Experience*, 27.

The Physics of Miraculous Healing

8 Spink, *Mother Teresa: A Complete Authorized Biography*, 39.
9 Yogananda. *Autobiography of a Yogi*, 97.
10 Dennis, *The Pattern*, 40.
11 Millman, *Divine Interventions: True Stories of Mystery and Miracles That Change Lives*, 108.
12 Ewing, "Do You Know About these 10 Amazing Miracles of Lourdes?"
13 Beliefnet, "Heaven Healed Me: 7 Miraculous Healings Doctors Can't Explain."
14 Woodrell, "3 Miracles at Lourdes (Approved and Scientifically Validated)."
15 Steiner, *How to Know Higher Worlds: A Modern Path of Initiation*, 36.
16 Yogananda, *How to Be a Success*, 79.
17 Williams, "Mellen-Thomas Benedict's Near-Death Experience."
18 Ritchie, *Return from Tomorrow*, 19.
19 Williams, "Juliet Nightingale's Near-Death Experience."
20 Hawkins, *Power vs. Force: The Hidden Determinants of Human Behavior*, 22.
21 Williams, "Dianne Morrissey's Near-Death Experience."

Chapter 10

1 Bihari, "How Medication Works in Your Body."
2 Siegel, *Love, Medicine and Miracles*, 22.
3 Good News Network, "Radical Remissions: 9 Ways People Have Beat Terminal Cancer."
4 Vogel, "150 Inspiring Quotes on Beating Cancer from Super Survivors."
5 Ibid.
6 Ibid.

Chapter 12

1 Siegel, *Love, Medicine and Miracles*, 76.
2 Yogananda, "Knowing God."
3 Aurobindo, *The Life Divine*, 97-99.

4 Yogananda, *The Essence of Self-Realization: The Wisdom of Paramhansa Yogananda*, 10, 9.
5 Barks, *The Essential Rumi*, 22.
6 Sivananda, "How to Find Peace of Mind."
7 Kriyananda, *Affirmations for Self-Healing*, 7, Security.
8 Kriyananda, *Affirmations for Self-Healing*, 44, Acceptance.
9 Kriyananda, *Affirmations for Self-Healing*, 15, Enthusiasm.
10 Wallace, *The Burning Within*, 95.

Chapter 13
1 Aitkenhead, "Buy Gatwick? Why Not?"
2 Emerson, *Emerson: The Ultimate Collection*, 213.
3 Csikszentmihalyi, *Flow: The Psychology of Optimal Experience*, 200.
4 Clark, *The Man Who Tapped the Secrets of the Universe*, Kindle Locations 227-231.
5 Kriyananda, *The Art and Science of Raja Yoga*, 258.
6 Clark, *The Man Who Tapped the Secrets of the Universe*, Kindle Locations 91-93.
7 Yogananda, *How to Be Happy All the Time*, 76.

Chapter 14
1 Yogananda, *How to Be Happy All the Time*, 67.
2 Siegel, *Love, Medicine and Miracles*, 20.
3 Hay, *You Can Heal Your Life*, 1.
4 Yogananda, *How to Achieve Glowing Health and Vitality*, 128.
5 Kriyananda, *Affirmations for Self-Healing*, 14, Good Health.
6 Yogananda, *Scientific Healing Affirmations*, 52.
7 Ibid.
8 Kriyananda, *Affirmations for Self-Healing*, 41, Positive Thinking.
9 Yogananda, *How to Achieve Glowing Health and Vitality*, 101.
10 Sivananda, "Cosmic Consciousness."
11 Yogananda, *Essence of the Bhagavad Gita*, 2:20.
12 Yogananda, *How to Achieve Glowing Health and Vitality*, 109.
13 Yogananda, "Understanding Death and Loss."

The Physics of Miraculous Healing

Chapter 15

1 Atwater, *Beyond the Light*, 142.

2 Tennyson, *The Major Works*, 520.

3 Lionel, *The Seduction of the Occult Path: Encounters on the Road to Inner Transformation*.

4 Russell, *Universal Law, Natural Science and Philosophy*, Prelude.

5 Eckhart, *Meister Eckhart*, 153.

6 Yogananda, *Journey to Self-Realization*, 113.

7 Bhaktivedanta, *Kṛṣṇa, the Supreme Personality of Godhead*, Introduction.

8 Williams, "Howard Storm's Near-Death Experience."

9 Yogananda, "Knowing God."

10 Barks, *The Essential Rumi*, Ch. 11: Union.

11 Yogananda, *The Essence of Self-Realization: The Wisdom of Paramhansa Yogananda*, 179.

12 Kriyananda, *Affirmations for Self-Healing*, 14, Good Health.

13 Yogananda, *Scientific Healing Affirmations*, 53-54.

BIBLIOGRAPHY

Aitkenhead, Decca. "Buy Gatwick? Why Not?" The Guardian, September 19, 2008.
theguardian.com/business/2008/sep/20/branson.interview

Atwater, P. M. H. *Beyond the light: what isn't being said about near-death experience,* Carol Pub. Group, 1994.

Aurobindo. *The Life Divine*, Dutton, 1951.

Barasch, Marc. "Psychology of the Miraculous," Psychology Today, 1994. www.psychologytoday.com/us/articles/199403/psychology-the-miraculous

Barks, Coleman. *The Essential Rumi*, Harper San Francisco, 1995.

Barrett, L. F. "Are Emotions Natural Kinds?" Perspectives on Psychological Science, March 2006. journals.sagepub.com/doi/abs/10.1111/j.1745-6916.2006.00003.x

Barrett, L. F. "The conceptual act theory: A précis," Emotion Review, September 2014. journals.sagepub.com/doi/abs/10.1177/1754073914534479

Beliefnet. "Heaven Healed Me: 7 Miraculous Healings Doctors Can't Explain." www.beliefnet.com/faiths/christianity/galleries/heaven-healed-me-7-miraculous-healings-doctors-cant-explain.aspx

Berman, Phillip L. *The Journey Home: What Near-Death Experiences and Mysticism Teach Us about the Gift of Life*, Pocket Books, 1996.

Besant, Annie. *Karma,* Theosophical Pub. House, 1918.

Bhaktivedanta. *Kṛṣṇa, the Supreme Personality of Godhead,* Bhativedanta Book Trust, 1972.

Bihari, Michael. "How Medication Works in Your Body," verywellhealth, December 5, 2020. www.verywellhealth.com/how-drugs-work-in-your-body-1124115

Bohm, David and B.J. Hiley. *The Undivided Universe*, Reprint edition, Routledge, 1995.

Born, Max. *The Restless Universe*, Dover Publications, 1951.

Braud, W.G, & Schlitz, M.J. "Consciousness Interactions with Remote Biological Systems: Anomalous Intentionality Effects," Subtle Energies, 1991, Vol.2(1).

British Society for Cell Biology, "Ribosome." bscb.org/learning-resources/softcell-e-learning/ribosome/

Carrel, Alexis. *Man, the Unknown*, Hamish Hamilton, 1942.

Chow, Denise. "Why Your DNA May Not Be Your Destiny," *LiveScience*, June 4, 2015. http://www.livescience.com/37135-dna-epigenetics-disease-research.html

Clark, Glen. *The Man Who Tapped the Secrets of the Universe*. Kindle Edition. 2014.

Connolly, Marshall. "World renown scientist says he has found proof of God! We may be living the the 'Matrix'," Catholic Online, June 8, 2016. http://www.catholic.org/news/technology/story.php?id=69335

Coons, Philip M. "Psychophysiologic Aspects of Multiple Personality Disorder, A Review. Dissociation." Ridgeview Institute and the International Society for the Study of Multiple Personality & Dissociation, Vol. 1, No. 1.

Csikszentmihalyi, Mihaly. *Flow: The Psychology of Optimal Experience*, Harper Perennial Modern Classics, 1990.

Cummiskey, Barbara. "Barabara Cummiskey: Her Astonding Victory," Guideposts, April 1965.

Dennis, Lynnclaire. *The Pattern*, Integral Pub. in association with Entagram Productions, 1997.

Dicarlo, Russell. "Conversations Toward a New World View: Exploring the Human Energy System." healthy.net/2019/08/26/exploring-the-human-energy-system/

Dossey, Larry, MD. "Brains and Beyond: The Unfolding Vision of Health and Healing," Science Direct, Volume 12, Issue 5, September–October 2016.

Durr, Hans-Peter. Television Interview, PM Magazine, May, 2007.

Eadie, Betty J., and Curtis Taylor. *Embraced by the Light*, Gold Leaf Press, 1992.

Eckhart, and Matthew Fox. *Meditations with Meister Eckhart*, Bear & Co., 1983.

Eckhart, Meister, C. de B. Evans, Franz Pfeiffer. *Meister Eckhart*, J.M. Watkins, 1952.

Einstein, Albert. *The World As I See It*, Philosophical Library, 1949.

Emerson, Ralph Waldo. *Emerson: The Ultimate Collection*. Titan Read. 2015.

Engel, Gregory S., et al. "Evidence for wavelike energy transfer through quantum coherence in photosynthetic systems," Nature, 446, (7137), April 12, 2007.

Ewing, Jeannie. "Do You Know About these 10 Amazing Miracles of Lourdes?" The Mystical Humanity of Christ Publishing. www.coraevans.com/blog/article/do-you-know-about-these-10-amazing-miracles-of-lourdes

Fielding, J. W. L., et al. "An interim report of a prospective, randomized, controlled study of adjuvant chemotherapy in operable gastric cancer: British stomach cancer group," World Journal of Surgery, 1983, 7 (3).

Folger, T. "Quantum Shmantum"; Discover 22:37-43, 2001.

Fowler, J. H. and N. A. Christakis. "Dynamic spread of happiness in a large social network: longitudinal analysis over 20 years in the Framingham Heart Study," BMJ, December 4, 2008.

Good News Network, "Radical Remissions: 9 Ways People Have Beat Terminal Cancer," May 6, 2014. www.goodnewsnetwork.org/top-9-healing-blows-to-cancer/

Goswami, Amit. *The Self-Aware Universe*, Putnam's Sons, 1993.

Hawkins, David R. *Power vs. Force: The Hidden Determinants of Human Behavior*, Veritas, 1995.

Hay, Louise. *You Can Heal Your Life*, Hay House, 2017.

Hildebrand, Ulrich. Translated. "Das Universum - Hinweis auf Gott?" No. 10, October 1988 *Ethos. Die Zeitschrift für die ganze Familie* 10.

Ho, Mae-Wan. "Bioenergetics and Biocommunication," 1996. www.ratical.org/co-globalize/MaeWanHo/biocom95.html

Hordern, A. "Psychopharmacology: Some historical considerations," in Joyce CRB, *Psychopharmacology: Dimensions and Perspectives*, Tavistock Publications Ltd, 1968.

Hoyle, Fred, and N. Chandra Wickramasinghe. *Evolution from Space*, J.M. Dent & Sons, 1981.

Jung, C. G. *Memories, Dreams, Reflections*, Pantheon Books, 1963.

Kastrup, "Coming to Grips with the Implications of Quantum Mechanics," Scientific American, May, 29, 2018. www.scientificamerican.com/blog/observations/coming-to-grips-with-the-implications-of-quantum-mechanics/

Klopfer, "Psychological Variables in Human Cancer," Journal of Prospective Techniques, 31, 1957.

Kriyananda. *Affirmations for Self-Healing*, Crystal Clarity Publishers, 2005.

———*The Art and Science of Raja Yoga*, Ananda Sangha, 2010.

LeShan, Lawrence. *Cancer as a Turning Point*, Penguin Publishing Group, 1994.

Lionel, Frédéric. *The Seduction of the Occult Path: Encounters on the Road to Inner Transformation*, Turnstone, 1983.

Livio, Fr. "Description of Heaven," http://www.medjugorje.com/medjugorje/heaven-purgatory-hell/613-description-of-heaven.html

Lourdes Medical Bureau, Wikipedia, https://en.wikipedia.org/wiki/Lourdes_Medical_Bureau, viewed March 2024.

Luparello, T., H. A. Lyons, E. R. Bleecker, et al. "Influences of Suggestion on Airway Reactivity in Asthmatic Subjects," Psychosomatic Medicine, 1996, vol. 30, no. 6.

Macrae, Norman. *The Scientific Genius Who Pioneered the Modern Computer, Game Theory, Nuclear Deterrence and Much More*, American Mathematical Society, 1992.

Martin, Laurelynn G. *Searching for Home: A Personal Journey of Transformation and Healing after a Near-Death Experience*, Cosmic Concepts, 1996.

Mayo Clinic, "Breast Cancer," Mayo Clinic Online. mayoclinic.org/diseases-conditions/breast-cancer/symptoms-causes/syc-20352470

Mayo Clinic, "High blood pressure (hypertension)," Mayo Clinic Online. mayoclinic.org/diseases-conditions/high-blood-pressure/symptoms-causes/syc-20373410

Millman, Dan. *Divine Interventions: True Stories of Mystery and Miracles That Change Lives*, Rodale, 2000.

Moorjani, Anita. *Dying to Be Me: My Journey from Cancer, to near Death, to True Healing*. 1st ed, Hay House, 2012.

Moseley JB, et al. "A controlled trial of arthroscopic surgery for osteoarthritis of the knee," The New England Journal of Medicine, 2002, 347 (2).

Nbcnews.com. "Survey: Most doctors believe in God, afterlife," 2005. www.nbcnews.com/health/health-news/survey-most-doctors-believe-god-afterlife-flna1C9442008

Ornish, D, M. J. Magbanua, G. Weidner, et al. "Changes in Prostate Gene Expression in Men Undergoing an Intensive Nutrition and Lifestyle Intervention," Proceedings of the National Academy of Sciences, vol. 105, no. 24, 2008.

Panitchayangkoon, Gitt, et al. "Long-lived quantum coherence in photosynthetic complexes at physiological temperature," Proceedings of the National Academy of Sciences, 107 (28), July 6, 2010.

Penman, Danny. "Could there be proof to the theory that we're ALL psychic?" Daily Mail, January 2008. www.dailymail.co.uk.

Planck, Max. "Das Wesen der Materie [The Nature of Matter]," a 1944 speech in Florence, Italy, Archiv zur Geschichte der Max-Planck-Gesellschaft, Abt. Va, Rep. 11 Planck, Nr. 1797

Popp, F.A. and Li, K.H. "Hyperbolic Relaxation as a Sufficient Condition of a Fully Coherent Ergodic Field," International Journal of Theoretical Physics, 32, 1993.

Price, Jan. *The Other Side of Death,* Fawcett Columbine, 1996.

Ritchie, George G. *Return from Tomorrow,* Chosen Books, revised edition, 2023.

Rönn, T., P. Volkov, C. Davegårdh, et al. "A Six Months Exercise Intervention Influences the Genome-Wide DNA Methylation Pattern in Human Adipose Tissue," *PLOS Genetics* vol. 9, no. 6: p. e1003572, 2013.

Russell, Walter, Lao Russell. *Universal Law, Natural Science and Philosophy*, The Walter Russell Foundation, 1950.

Segerstrom, S. C. et al. "Psychological Stress and the Human Immune System: A Meta-Analytic Study of 30 Years of Inquiry." Psychological Bulletin, 2004, 130(4): 601-630. pubmed.ncbi.nlm.nih.gov/15250815/

Shepard, K.R. & Braun, B.G. "Visual changes in multiple personality," *PROCEEDINGS OF THE SECOND INTERNATIONAL CONFERENCE ON MULTIPLE PERSONALITY/DISSOCIATIVE STATES,* Rush-Presbyterian-St Luke's Medical Center, 1985.

Siegel, Bernie S, MD. *Love, Medicine and Miracles*, William Morrow Paperbacks, 2011.

Sivananda. "How to Find Peace of Mind," The Divine Life Society. sivanandaonline.org/?cmd=displaysection&section_id=848&format=html.

———"Cosmic Consciousness," The Divine Life Society. http://www.sivanandaonline.org/public_html/?cmd=displaysection&section_id=1727

The Physics of Miraculous Healing

Smith, Jayne. "Moment of Truth: A Window On Life After Death," Video transcript, Starpath Productions, 1987.

Spink, Kathryn. *Mother Teresa: A Complete Authorized Biography,* Harper San Francisco, 1997.

Spurgin, Nora M. *Insights into the Afterlife: 30 Questions on What to Expect,* Womans Federation of World Peace, 1994.

Stein, R. "Happiness can spread among people like a contagion, study indicates," *Washington Post online,* December 5, 2009. www.washingtonpost.com.

Steiner, Rudolf, and Christopher Bamford. *How to Know Higher Worlds: A Modern Path of Initiation*, Hudson, Anthroposophic Press, 1994.

St. Maarten, Anton. *Divine Living: The Essential Guide to Your True Destiny.* Indigo House. 2012.

Strasburger, "Sight and blindness in the same person: Gating in the visual system," PsyCh Journal, December, 2015, 4.

Susskind, L. *The Black Hole war – My Battle with Steven Hawking to Make the World Safe for Quantum Mechanics,* Little, Brown and Company, 2008.

Suzuki, Daisetz Teitaro. *Zen and Japanese Culture,* Pantheon Books, 1959.

Swedenborg, Emanuel and George F. Dole. *Heaven and Hell,* Swedenborg Foundation, 1984.

Swimme, Brian. *The Hidden Heart of the Cosmos,* Orbis Books, 1996.

Tennyson, Alfred and Roberts, Adam. *The Major Works,* Oxford University Press, 2009.

Thomas, Lewis. *The Youngest Science: Notes of a Medicine Watcher,* Viking Press, 1983.

Thompson, Eric. "Scientific Evidence for a Connecting Matrix: An Introduction to Biofield Science, Part 2." Iawake. www.iawaketechnologies.com

Vaillant, G. E., "Natural history of male psychologic health: effects of mental health on physical health," New England Journal of Medicine, Dec 6, 1979, 301(23):1249-54. pubmed.ncbi.nlm.nih.gov/503127/

Vogel, Kaitlin. "150 Inspiring Quotes on Beating Cancer from Super Survivors," Parade, December 23, 2020. parade.com/1140135/kaitlin-vogel/cancer-quotes/

Wallace, RaNelle and Curtis Taylor. *The Burning Within*, Gold Leaf Press, 1994.

Wiener, Norbert. *The Human Use of Human Beings,* Avon Books, 1954.

Williams, Kevin. "Christian Andreason's Near Death Experience," NDE, September 20, 2019. near-death.com/christian-andreason-nde/

——— "Dianne Morrissey's Near-Death Experience," NDE, September 16, 2019. near-death.com/dianne-morrissey/

——— "Howard Storm's Near-Death Experience," NDE, September 26, 2019. near-death.com/howard-storm-nde/

——— "Juliet Nightingale's Near-Death Experience," NDE, September 18, 2019. near-death.com/juliet-nightingale/

——— "Mellen-Thomas Benedict's Near-Death Experience," NDE, September 18, 2019. near-death.com/mellen-thomas-benedict/

Woodrell, Lauren. "3 Miracles at Lourdes (Approved and Scientifically Validated)," Magis Center, February, 2024. www.magiscenter.com/blog/miracles-at-lourdes

Yogananda, Paramhansa and J. Donald Walters. *The Essence of Self-Realization: The Wisdom of Paramhansa Yogananda,* Crystal Clarity Publishers, 1990.

Yogananda, Paramhansa and Kriyananda, Swami. *Essence of the Bhagavad Gita*, Crystal Clarity Publishers, 2006.

Yogananda, *Autobiography of a Yogi*, (reprint of original Theosophical Library 1946 edition), Nevada City, CA: Crystal Clarity Publishers, 2005.

———"The Astral World," Self-Realization Magazine, Spring/Summer, 2010.

———*How to Achieve Glowing Health and Vitality*, Crystal Clarity Publishers, 2011.

———*How to Awaken Your True Potential*, Crystal Clarity Publishers, 2016.

———*How to Be a Success*, Crystal Clarity Publishers, 2008.

———*How to Be Happy All the Time*, Crystal Clarity Publishers, 2006.

———*Journey to Self-Realization*, Self-Realization Fellowship, 2000.

——— "Knowing God." Self-Realization Fellowship. yogananda.org/knowing-god.

———*Scientific Healing Affirmations*, Self-Realization Fellowship, 1990.

———*The Second Coming of Christ: the Resurrection of the Christ Within You: A Revelatory Commentary on the Original Teachings of Jesus*, Self-Realization Fellowship, 2004.

——— "Understanding Death and Loss," Self-Realization Fellowship. yogananda.org/understanding-death-and-loss

———*Where There is Light*, Self-Realization Fellowship, 1988.

———*Whispers from Eternity*, Crystal Clarity Publishers, 2008.

The Physics of Miraculous Healing

ACKNOWLEDGMENTS

I could not have begun to understand the unity of science and spirituality that lies behind the human body if it weren't for the teachings of Paramhansa Yogananda. Though Indian by birth, Yogananda lived and taught in the west for over thirty years. In his writings you will find an insightful respect for science and in his world-famous 1946 work, *Autobiography of a Yogi*, he devotes two chapters to exploring the intersections of science with spirituality. In his writings he often used concepts and terms from physics, chemistry, neuroscience, biology, psychology, medicine, and other scientific disciplines to support and clarify profound spiritual truths. Sometimes referred to as the father of yoga and meditation in the west, I believe he is also the father of the emerging new unity of science and spirituality.

This book would not be possible without the generous help of many people. Prakash Van Cleave's long hours exercising his editing prowess on my prose makes me appear to be a far better writer than I actually am. Bob Stolzman's eagle-eye insured a clear, readable text and layout. The exquisite beauty of the cover is due to the creative design skills of Phil Dyer, a long-time friend and collaborator. My wife deserves a special mention for being my first reader. She has helped me immeasurably to shape the way I've presented the complex content at the heart of this book. If you found it easy to understand, send her a mental thank you.

Lastly, I'd like to thank the many people who, having read this or my other books, have been moved to communicate to me their appreciation via social media, book reviews, or emails. Authors necessarily work in isolation. We rarely get applause. Being told by readers that they were inspired, enlightened, moved, or benefitted in some way from my books is a precious accolade.

ABOUT THE AUTHOR

A polymath, Joseph Selbie is known for creating bridges of understanding between the modern evidenced-based discoveries of science and the timeless experience-based discoveries of the mystics. He is also the author of *The Physics of God*, a unification of science and religion; *Break Through the Limits of the Brain*, neuroscientific support for spiritual experience; and *The Yugas*, a factual look at India's tradition of cyclical history.

In demand as a presenter he has appeared on many programs including: The Chopra Well with Deepak Chopra, Coast to Coast with George Noory, Gaia's Open Minds with Regina Meredith, and Buddha at the Gas Pump with Rick Archer. He was nominated *Trailblazer of the Decade* by Om Times Magazine and appears with Elizabeth Rohm in the 2014 docudrama, *Finding Happiness*.

A dedicated Kriya yoga meditator for over fifty years, he has taught yoga, meditation, and universal experiential spirituality throughout the US and Europe. In 1975 Joseph became a member of Ananda, a spiritual movement inspired by the teachings of Paramhansa Yogananda, author of *Autobiography of a Yogi*.

www.josephselbie.com

www.ingramcontent.com/pod-product-compliance
Lightning Source LLC
Chambersburg PA
CBHW070602010526
44118CB00012B/1431